Paul's Letters to the
GALATIANS, EPHESIANS, PHILIPPIANS, & COLOSSIANS

The MorningStar Vision Bible

by Rick Joyner

MorningStar Publications

Paul's Letters to the Galatians, Ephesians, Philippians, & Colossians
by Rick Joyner
Copyright © 2014
Trade Size Edition

Distributed by MorningStar Publications, Inc.,
a division of MorningStar Fellowship Church
375 Star Light Drive, Fort Mill, SC 29715
www.MorningStarMinistries.org
1-800-542-0278

International Standard Book Number— 978-1-60708-548-5; 1-60708-548-8

Cover Design: Kevin Lepp and Kandi Evans
Book Layout: Kevin Lepp and Kandi Evans

Unless otherwise indicated, all Scripture quotations are taken from the New American Standard Bible, copyright © 1960, 1962, 1963, 1968, 1971, 1973, 1974, 1977 by The Lockman Foundation. Italics in Scripture are for emphasis only.

No part of this book may be reproduced or transmitted in any form or by any means, electronic, or mechanical, including photocopying, recording, or by any information storage and retrieval system, without written permission from the author.

All rights reserved.
Printed in the United States of America.

For a free catalog of MorningStar Resources,
please call 1-800-542-0278.

Paul's Letters
Table of Contents

Preface 5

Galatians
Introduction 11
Chapter 1 13
Chapter 2 17
Chapter 3 21
Chapter 4 25
Chapter 5 29
Chapter 6 33
Proper Names and Definitions 37

Ephesians
Introduction 39
Chapter 1 43
Chapter 2 47
Chapter 3 51
Chapter 4 55
Chapter 5 60
Chapter 6 65
Proper Names and Definitions 69

Philippians
Introduction 71
Chapter 1 73
Chapter 2 79
Chapter 3 83
Chapter 4 87
Proper Names and Definitions 91

Colossians

Introduction	....	93
Chapter 1	....	94
Chapter 2	....	98
Chapter 3	....	101
Chapter 4	....	105
Proper Names and Definitions	....	107

PREFACE
THE MORNINGSTAR VISION BIBLE
BY RICK JOYNER

Next to His Son and the Holy Spirit, The Bible is God's greatest gift to mankind. What treasure on earth could be compared to one Word from God? There is good reason why The Bible is the bestselling book of all time by such a wide margin. The importance of The Bible cannot be overstated. If Jesus, who is the Word, would take His stand on the written Word when challenged by the devil, how much more must we be established on that Word to take our stand and live our lives by it?

The most basic purpose of **The MorningStar Vision Bible** is accuracy and faithfulness to the intended meaning of the Author, the Holy Spirit. His written Word reveals the path to life, salvation, transformation, deliverance, and healing for every soul who would seek to know God. The universe is upheld by the Word of His power, so there is no stronger foundation that we could ever build our lives on other than His Word. Therefore, we have pursued this project with the utmost care in that what is presented here is His Word and not ours. We were very careful not to let anyone work on it that had an agenda other than a love for the truth and the deepest respect for the fact that we were handling this most precious treasure—God's own Word.

The primary accuracy of any translation is its adherence to the original text in the original languages The Bible was written in, Hebrew and Greek. However, there are problems when you try to translate from a language such as Greek into a language like English because Greek is so much more expressive than English. For example, there are several different Greek words with different meanings that are translated as one word "love" in our English version. The Greek words distinguish between such things as friendship love, erotic attraction, or unconditional love. When we just translate these as "love," it may be generally true, but something basic in what the Author tried to convey is left out. As we mature in Christ by following the Spirit, these deeper, more specific meanings become important. Therefore, we have sought to include the nuances of the Greek language in this version.

A basic biblical guide we used for this work was Psalm 12:6: **"The words of the Lord are pure words; as silver tried in a furnace on the earth, refined seven times."** Every Book we release of this version has been through a meticulous process at least seven times to ensure faithfulness to the original intent. Even so, we do not yet consider this to be a completed work. We are releasing these Book by Book in softcover to seek even further examination by those who read them. We are asking our readers to send us challenges for any word, phrase, or part that you think may not be accurate, along with your reasons. These will be received, considered, and researched with openness. If you have insights that you think should be added to the commentary, we will consider those as well.

You can email these or any comments that you have to bible@morningstarministries.org, or mail them to us at:

MorningStar Publications
375 Star Light Drive
Fort Mill, South Carolina 29715

Please include any credentials that you might have that would be relevant, but they are not necessary for this.

My personal credentials for compiling and editing such a work are first my love for The Bible and my respect for its integrity. I have been a Christian for more than forty years, and I have read The Bible through from cover to cover at least once a year. I do have an earned doctorate in theology from a good, accredited school, but have not used the title because I want my message received on the merits of its content, not by a title. Though I have been in pursuit of knowing the Lord and His Word for more than forty years, I still feel more comfortable thinking of myself as a student rather than an expert. If that bothers you, I understand, but when handling the greatest truth the world has ever known, I feel we must be as humble and transparent as possible.

Most of those who have worked on this project with me have been students at MorningStar University. This is a unique school that has had students from ages sixteen to over eighty. Some have been remarkably skilled in languages, especially Hebrew and Greek. Some have been believers and students of the Word for a long time. Others were fairly new to the faith, but were strong and devoted to seeking and knowing the truth. These were the ones that I was especially interested in recruiting for this project because of the Lord's statement in Matthew 11:25:

> **At that time Jesus answered and said, "I praise You, O Father, Lord of heaven and earth, that You did hide these things from the wise and intelligent and did reveal them to babes."**

Because **"God resists the proud, but gives grace to the humble"** (see James 4:6; I Peter 5:5 NKJV), the humility of a relatively young believer can be more important for discerning truth than great knowledge and experience if these have caused us to become proud.

Also, as Peter stated concerning Paul's writings in II Peter 3:15-16:

> **Paul, according to the wisdom given him, wrote to you,**
>
> **as also in all his letters, speaking in them of these things, in which are some things hard to understand, which the untaught and unstable distort, as they do also the rest of the Scriptures, to their own destruction.**

So the untaught can be prone to distort the truth if they are also unstable. This is why the relatively young believers that I sought to be a part of our team were not just stable but strong in the Lord and their resolve to know the truth.

Even so, not everyone who has great knowledge and experience has become so proud that it causes God to resist them. Those who have matured and yet remained humble and teachable may be some of the greatest treasures we have in the body of Christ. Such elders are certainly worthy of great honor and should be listened to and heeded. Nowhere in Scripture are we exhorted to honor the youth, but over and over we are commanded to honor the elders.

So it seems we have a paradox—the Lord reveals His ways to babes, but elders are the ones responsible for keeping His people on the path of life, walking in His ways. This is not a contradiction. As with many of the paradoxes in Scripture, the tension between the extremes is intended to help keep us on the path of life by giving us boundaries. Pride in our experience and knowledge can cause us to stray from this path, as can our lack of knowledge if it is combined with instability. The vision and exuberance of youth are needed to keep the fire of passion for the Lord and His ways burning. This is why the Lord said that the wise brought forth from their treasures things both new and old (see Matthew 13:52).

For this reason, I sought the young in the faith who are also stable and displayed a discipline and devotion to obedience to the truth. I also sought the contributions of the experienced and learned who continued to have the humility to whom God gives His grace. As far as Greek and Hebrew scholars, I was more interested in those who are technically-minded, devoted to details, and who seemed to be free of doctrinal prejudices.

This is not to give the impression that all who worked on this project went over the entire Bible. I did have some who went over the entire New Testament, but most only worked on a single Book, and sometimes just a single issue. I may not have told many of the Greek and Hebrew experts that it was for this project when I inquired about a matter with them.

I realize that this is a unique way to develop a Bible version, but as we are told in I Corinthians 13:12 we "see in part" and **"know in part."** Therefore, we all need to put what we have together with what others have if we are going to have a complete picture. This version is the result of many years of labor by many people. Having been a publisher for many years, I know every editor or proofreader will tend to catch different things, and so it has been with this project. We also realize that as hard as we have worked on being as accurate as possible, we may have missed some things, and we will be genuinely appreciative of every one that is caught by our readers. Again, our goal is to have the most accurate English version of The Bible possible.

Even though accuracy and faithfulness to the original intent of the Holy Spirit were our most basic devotions, we also sought insights that could come from many other factors, such as the culture of the times in which the different Books of The Bible were written. Along with myself, many other contributors have spent countless hours of research examining words, phrases, the authors of the Books of The Bible, their times, and even the history of cities and places mentioned in it. Though the knowledge gained by this research did not affect the words in the text of The Bible, they sometimes gave a greater illumination and depth to their meaning that was profound. Sometimes they made obscure, hard to comprehend phrases come to life.

One of the obvious intents of the Author was to be able to communicate to any seeker of truth on the level they are on. For the most basic seeker, knowing such things as the nuances or more detailed meaning of the Greek or Hebrew words may not be important. As we mature, we will seek deeper understanding if we follow the Holy Spirit. We are told in I Corinthians 2:10, **"For to us God revealed them through the Spirit; for the Spirit searches all things, even the depths of God."** Therefore, those who follow the Spirit will not be shallow in their understanding of anything and will especially search to know the depths of the nature of God.

Our single greatest hope is that **The MorningStar Vision Bible** will accurately reveal the will and intent of the Lord, and compel all who read it to love Him more, which is the chief purpose of man. If we love Him more, we will then begin to love one another more. As we grow in love, we will also grow in our devotion to know Him even more, know His ways, and do the things that please Him. He deserves this from us more than could ever be expressed.

There is nothing greater than knowing Him. I am convinced that anything we learn about God will make us love Him more, which is our chief purpose and the one thing that will determine if we are successful human beings. This is also the only thing that can lead to the true peace and true joy that is beyond anything this world can supply. There is no greater adventure that can be had in this life than the true Christian life. The Bible is the map to the greatest quest and the greatest adventure that we could ever experience.

Introduction
Paul's Letter to the Galatians

Galatia was not a city, but an entire region in Asia Minor. For this reason, Paul addresses this letter to "the churches of Galatia" (see Galatians 1:2; 3:1). This region was also sometimes referred to as Gallogriecia because of its Gallic and Celtic conquerors and settlers that dominated the region as the ruling aristocracy during this period.

Most theologians fix the date of this Epistle shortly after the apostle's second visit to Galatia, on or about A.D.51.

The Epistle is written in three basic parts. The first is apologetic. In the first two chapters, the apostle gives personal reasons why he is qualified to address the great issues he will take up in this letter.

The second part is polemical. Paul establishes the foundational truths of the crucial doctrine of salvation, which is by the grace of God through faith in Christ. This is the cardinal truth of Christianity, and Paul makes the strongest case found in the New Testament for this in chapters three and four.

The third part, chapters five and six, is an exhortation to the Galatians to stand fast in their freedom, warning them not to void their union with Christ by succumbing to false teachings that would bring them under the yoke of the law. Paul also exhorts them not to use their freedom to do deeds of the flesh, which would nullify their inheritance in the kingdom of God. In this he is warning them against the extremes on either side of life's path—legalism on one side and lawlessness on the other. Either of these could cost them their inheritance in Christ. The answer is to live by the Spirit that has been given to them, which is the power to live by love for God and love for one another. From the beginning of the New Covenant in the first century, navigating between these extremes is the challenge of every believer, church, and movement.

The brief but concise Epistle to the Galatians is the most powerful discourse ever written to help us stay on the path of life between the extremes that would carry us away from Christ. For this reason, it is crucial to the New Testament and should be read regularly to help us stay on the path of life.

Paul's Letter to The GALATIANS

Galatians 1

Salutation

1 Paul, an apostle not sent by men, neither through the agency of man, but through Jesus Christ, and God the Father, who raised Him from the dead,

2 and all the brethren that are with me, to the churches in Galatia:

3 Grace to you, and peace, from God the Father, and our Lord Jesus Christ,

4 who gave Himself for our sins, that He might deliver us out of this present evil world, according to the will of our God and Father:

5 to whom be the glory for ever and ever. Amen.

A Different Gospel

6 I marvel that you are so quickly departing from Him who called you through the grace of Christ for a different gospel,

7 which is not another gospel, only there are some that trouble you, and would pervert the gospel of Christ.

8 If we, or an angel from heaven, should preach to you any gospel other than that which we preached to you, let him be accursed.

9 As we have stated, and now I say again, if any man preaches to you a gospel other than that which you received, let him be accursed.

10 For am I now seeking the favor of men, or of God? Or am I striving to please men? If I were still trying to please men I would not be a bondservant of Christ.

GALATIANS 1:11 - GALATIANS 1:24

Paul's Quest for The Truth

11 For I make known to you, brethren, about the gospel that was preached by me, that it is not from man.

12 For neither did I receive it from man, nor was I taught it by man, but it came to me through a revelation of Jesus Christ.

13 For you have heard of my manner of life in times past in Judaism, how I persecuted the church of God worse than anyone else, and tried to destroy it.

14 I advanced in Judaism beyond many of my contemporaries, being more exceedingly zealous for the traditions of my fathers.

15 When it was the good pleasure of God, who separated me even from my mother's womb, and called me through His grace,

16 to reveal His Son in me, that I might preach Him among the Gentiles, I did not immediately consult with men,

17 and neither did I go up to Jerusalem to those who were apostles before me. I went away into Arabia, and again I returned to Damascus.

18 Then after three years I went up to Jerusalem to visit Cephas, and stayed with him for fifteen days.

19 I did not see the other apostles, except James the Lord's brother.

20 Now concerning the things that I write to you, before God I testify that I do not lie.

21 Then I went into the regions of Syria and Cilicia.

22 I was still not recognized by the churches of Judaea which were in Christ,

23 but they only heard, "He that once persecuted us now preaches the faith that he once tried to destroy,"

24 and they glorified God because of me.

Salutation

Galatians 1:1-5: This is Paul's typical salutation. He always identifies himself and his ministry, then gives his blessing of grace and peace that is ours through the cross of Jesus. This

begins the communication with the first, and most important, point of our relationship with one another—our redemption through Christ.

A Different Gospel

1:6-10: The apostle, a little uncharacteristically, confronts his readers very quickly. This indicates the gravity with which he viewed their falling to the deception of a false teaching: one that perverts the basic gospel truth of the cross and seeks to bring believers under the yoke of the law. To this day, this false teaching perverts the lives of many believers. Confronting this is the primary reason for this Epistle.

In verse 10, Paul boldly states that if he were still seeking the approval of men, he would not be a bondservant of Christ. To the degree that we are controlled by what people think, we have likely compromised our service to the King. This one issue probably causes more leaders to divert from the way of truth than any other factor.

Paul's Quest for The Truth

1:11-24: The apostle reminds the Galatians how he received and confirmed the gospel he preached to them—a gospel that, by then, was well-known throughout the empire. He continues to recount how he, who once persecuted the church, has now devoted himself to building it. He, the "Pharisee of Pharisees," one of the most vehement defenders of the law and the traditions, was now the chief apostle of the grace of God. Paul had better credentials than anyone for addressing the subject of this letter—the conflict between law and grace that remains to this day and is so critical to the promulgation of the New Covenant.

NOTES

Paul's Letter to the
GALATIANS
Galatians 2

The Confirmation of Paul's Message

1 Then, after the fourteen years, I went up again to Jerusalem with Barnabas, taking Titus with me.

2 I went up because of a revelation, so I laid before them the gospel that I preach among the Gentiles, but privately before those who were of reputation, unless by any means I should be running, or had run, in vain.

3 But not even Titus who was with me, being a Greek, was compelled to be circumcised.

4 It was because of the false brethren who secretly entered in, and who came in secretly to spy out our liberty that we have in Christ Jesus, that they might bring us into bondage,

5 to whom we gave no place, nor did we submit to them for even one hour, so that the truth of the gospel might continue with you.

6 Those who were of reputation (what they were does not matter to me because God is not a respecter of persons), imparted nothing to me.

7 When they saw that I had been entrusted with the gospel to the uncircumcision, even as Peter was with the gospel to the circumcision

8 (for he that worked in Peter for the apostleship to the circumcision worked in me also for the Gentiles),

9 and when they perceived the grace that was given to me, James and Cephas and John, those who were reputed to be pillars, gave to me

and Barnabas the right hands of fellowship, so that we should go to the Gentiles, and they to the circumcision.

10 They only asked us to remember the poor, which I was also zealous to do.

Paul Rebukes Peter

11 However, when Cephas came to Antioch I challenged him to his face because he stood condemned.

12 Before certain men came from James he ate with the Gentiles, but when they came, he drew back and separated himself, fearing those who were of the circumcision.

13 Then the rest of the Jews drew back with him, so that even Barnabas was carried away with their hypocrisy.

14 When I saw that they were not being straightforward about the truth of the gospel, I said to Cephas in front of them all, "If you, being a Jew live as the Gentiles do, and not as the Jews, how do you compel the Gentiles to live as the Jews?"

Law or Grace

15 We are Jews in the natural, and not sinners from the Gentiles,

16 yet knowing that a man is not justified by the works of the law, but through faith in Jesus Christ, even we believed on Christ Jesus that we might be justified by faith in Christ, and not by the works of the law because by the works of the law no one will be justified.

17 If, while we sought to be justified in Christ, we ourselves also were found sinners, is Christ a minister of sin? God forbid.

18 For if I build up again those things that I destroyed I prove myself to be a transgressor.

19 For through the law I died to the law that I might live to God.

20 I have been crucified with Christ, and therefore it is no longer I who lives, but Christ lives in me. The life that I now live in the flesh I live by faith in the Son of God, who loved me, and gave Himself for me.

21 I do not make void the grace of God, for if righteousness is through the law then Christ died for nothing.

The Confirmation of Paul's Message

Galatians 2:1-10: The apostle establishes how his message was authenticated and recognized by the counsel of apostles and elders in Jerusalem. This is important in establishing his authority to verify the doctrines of the church which he intends to do through this letter.

Paul Rebukes Peter

2:11-14: Paul explains how the law and fear of man caused even Cephas (Peter) to fall to the terrible sin of racism, separating himself from his Gentile brethren in Christ for the sake of appearances. Paul, the youngest of the apostles at the time, had the courage to rebuke Peter openly for this transgression because of its most destructive implications for the gospel.

Law or Grace

2:15-21: Paul makes the crucial point that if we seek justification through the law, then we are renouncing the grace of God gained for us by the cross of Jesus. It is not possible to live by both New Covenant redeeming grace paid for by Christ and our own righteousness by the law. This conflict must be settled in the heart of every believer. It is one or the other, but can never be both.

NOTES

Paul's Letter to The
GALATIANS
Galatians 3

Law or Spirit

1 O foolish Galatians, who bewitched you, before whose eyes Jesus Christ was openly exhibited as crucified?

2 This one thing I would like to learn from you: did you receive the Spirit by the works of the law, or by hearing with faith?

3 Are you so foolish that, having begun in the Spirit, are you now trying to be perfected by the flesh?

4 Did you suffer so many things in vain, if indeed it proves to be in vain.

5 Does He that gave you the Spirit, and works miracles among you, does He do it because of your works keeping the law, or because of your faith?

6 Even as Abraham believed God, and it was reckoned to him for righteousness,

7 know that it is those who are of faith who are the sons of Abraham.

8 The Scriptures, foreseeing that God would justify the Gentiles by faith, preached the gospel beforehand to Abraham, saying, **"In you shall all the nations be blessed"** (see Genesis 12:3).

9 So then it is those who are of faith who are the blessed with the faith of Abraham.

10 For as many as depend on the works of the law are under a curse because it is written, **"Cursed is everyone who does not continue to keep all things that are written in the book of the law, to do them"** (see Deuteronomy 27:26).

11 That no man is justified by the law before God is evident as it says, **"The righteous shall live by faith"** (see Habakkuk 2:4),

12 and the law is not of faith; but, **"He that does them shall live by them"** (see Leviticus 18:5).

13 Christ redeemed us from the curse of the law, having become a curse for us, as it is written, **"Cursed is every one that hangs on a tree"** (see Deuteronomy 21:23),

14 so that upon the Gentiles might become the blessing of Abraham in Christ Jesus, that we might receive the promise of the Spirit through faith.

15 Brethren, I speak now about the customs of men, though they are but a man's covenant, yet when one has been confirmed no one nullifies it, or adds to it.

The Law or The Promise

16 Now the promises were given to Abraham and to his seed. He does not say, **"And to seeds,"** as if there were many, but to one, **"And to your seed,"** (see Genesis 13:15,17:8) which is Christ.

17 Now this I say, a covenant confirmed beforehand by God, the law, that came four hundred and thirty years after the covenant given to Abraham, does not annul the first covenant so as to make the first promise of no effect.

18 For if the inheritance is attained by works, keeping the law, it is no longer a gift, or inheritance, but God granted it to Abraham by promise.

19 What then is the law? It was added because of transgressions, until the seed should come to whom the promise has been made, ordained as it was through angels by the hand of a mediator.

The Law as a Teacher

20 Now a mediator is not a mediator for just one person, but God is one.

21 Is the law then contrary to the promises of God? God forbid! If there had been a law given that could give life righteousness would

have been through the law *and there would have been no need of the cross.*

22 But the Scriptures shut up all under sin so that the promise by faith in Jesus Christ might be given to those who believe.

23 Before faith came, we were kept in subjection under the law, shut out of the faith that would afterwards be revealed.

24 In this way the law became our tutor to prepare us for Christ so that we might be justified by faith.

25 Now that faith has come we are no longer under a tutor.

26 For you are all sons of God through faith in Christ Jesus.

No Divisions in Christ

27 For as many of you as were baptized into Christ put on Christ.

28 There can be neither Jew nor Greek, neither bond nor free, nor male or female, for you all are one in Christ Jesus.

29 If you are Christ's, then you are Abraham's seed, heirs according to promise.

Law or Spirit

Galatians 3:1-15: This is the most clear, concise teaching in the Scriptures on the difference between Old Covenant law and New Covenant faith. Understanding this point is crucial to staying on the path of life. It is the amazing grace of God that one who was the "Pharisee of Pharisees," once the chief of the legalists, would become the most important champion of this essential truth. This remains one of the all-time great examples of the power of grace through the cross.

The Law or The Promise

3:16-19: We see that the promises of God are not to us individually, but to Christ. They are ours as we are in Christ. Christ is also the Promised Seed of Abraham. The ultimate,

all-encompassing covenant of God is the one begun through Abraham and consummated in Christ.

The Law as a Teacher

3:20-26: This is a clear articulation of the purpose of the law—to reveal to all who try to live by the law that it cannot be done. We need both the grace and empowerment of Christ to live by the righteous standards of God.

The apostle also makes the crucial point that if righteousness could be attained by the law, then there was no need for the Redeemer to come and go to the cross, which would have made the greatest event in history the most useless and foolish. For this reason, there is no other way to be reconciled to God except through the cross of Jesus.

No Divisions in Christ

3:27-29: If our identity is truly in Christ, then it will eclipse any other identity we have: cultural, racial, national, and even male or female.

NOTES

Paul's Letter to The GALATIANS
Galatians 4

Maturity Through the Son

1 Even when the heir is a child, in certain ways he does not differ from a bondservant even though he is to be lord of all.

2 They are placed under guardians and stewards until the day appointed by the father.

3 So we also, when we were children, were held in bondage under the elementary principles of the world,

4 but when the fullness of the time came, God sent forth His Son, born of a woman, born under the law,

5 that He might redeem those who were under the law, that we might receive the adoption of sons.

6 Because you are sons, God sent forth the Spirit of His Son into our hearts, crying, "Abba, Father."

7 So that you are no longer a bondservant, but a son, and if a son, then an heir through God.

Why Leave the Family to Become a Slave?

8 Even so, at that time, not knowing God, you were in bondage to those who are by nature are not gods,

9 but now that you have come to know God, and to be known by God, how do you turn back again to the weak and inferior elementary ways. Do you desire to be in bondage again?

10 Because you observe days, and months, and seasons, and years

11 I am afraid for you, because it seems that I may have labored for you in vain.

12 I beseech you, brethren, become as I am, for I also have become as you are. You never did me any harm,

Paul's Flesh a Trial

13 but you know that it was because of a weakness of the flesh that I preached the gospel to you the first time,

14 and that which was a trial for you in the condition of my flesh you overlooked, and did not despise, nor reject me, but you received me as if I were an angel from God, even as Christ Jesus.

15 Where then is that grace that you had? For I bear you witness that, if possible, you would have plucked out your eyes and given them to me.

16 So then have I now become your enemy by telling you the truth?

17 They zealously seek you with evil intentions. They desire to shut you out by becoming exclusive so that you will seek them.

18 But it is good to be zealously sought in the right way at all times, and not only when I am present with you.

Apostolic Travail

19 My little children, with whom I am again in travail until Christ is formed in you!

20 I wish I could be present with you now, and to change my tone, because I am perplexed about you.

21 Tell me, you that desire to be under the law, do you not understand the law?

Sarah and Hagar Are Types

22 For it is written, that Abraham had two sons, one by the bondwoman, and one by the freewoman.

23 The son by the bondwoman is born after the flesh, but the son by the freewoman is the heir of the promise.

24 These are an allegory, for these women represent the two covenants. The one represents Mount Sinai, bearing children under bondage, which is Hagar.

25 Now this Hagar is Mount Sinai in Arabia and represents the present Jerusalem, because she is in bondage with her children.

26 The Jerusalem that is above is free, which is our mother.

27 For it is written, **"Rejoice, you who are barren that have no children. Break forth and cry out, you that do not travail. For more are the children of the desolate than of her that has the husband"** (see Isaiah 54:1).

28 Now we, brethren, are as Isaac was, the children of promise.

29 But as he that was born after the flesh persecuted him that was born after the Spirit, so it is now.

30 What does the Scripture say? **"Cast out the bondwoman and her son; for the son of the bondwoman shall not be an heir with the son of the freewoman"** (see Genesis 21:10).

31 Therefore, brethren, we are not children of a bondwoman, but of the freewoman.

Maturity Through the Son

Galatians 4:1-7: True spiritual maturity is to grow up into Christ Jesus. He is also our righteousness. If we claim this, then we should never again stoop to seeking our own righteousness by the law or any other standard.

Why Leave the Family to Become a Slave?

4:8-12: If we return to the law for righteousness, we have renounced our inheritance in Christ as members of God's family in order to become slaves again. We have renounced our inheritance as sons and daughters of the King.

Paul's Flesh a Trial and Apostolic Travail

4:13-21: People often form exclusive clubs or sects to promote their superiority over others, causing others to seek them out. Paul asserts that this was the evil motive of those who were promoting the law as their basis of righteousness.

Sarah and Hagar Are Types

4:22-31: This is the most troublesome text to those who hold to the belief that all Scripture must be interpreted literally, with no allegory. This is a basic allegory with vast implications. If there is such metaphorical meaning to the story of Sarah and Hagar, then how much more is there in the other biblical accounts? Therefore, allegory is, by this text, established as an acceptable means of interpreting Scripture. However, that is not an excuse to cast off the literal meaning or sound exegesis that will keep us moored to the truth. Neither does it mean that every biblical account has an allegorical interpretation.

NOTES

Paul's Letter to The GALATIANS
Galatians 5

Legalism Severs From Christ

1 It was for freedom that Christ set us free. Stand fast therefore, and do not be entangled again with a yoke of bondage.

2 Take notice that I, Paul, say to you, that if you receive circumcision, Christ will be of no benefit to you.

3 Yes, I testify again to every man that receives circumcision, that he is obligated to keep the whole law.

4 You are severed from Christ if you seek to be justified by the law; you have fallen from grace.

5 For we, through the Spirit by faith, wait for the hope of righteousness.

6 For in Christ Jesus neither circumcision nor un-circumcision accomplishes anything, but faith working through love.

7 You were running well; who hindered you that you should not obey the truth?

8 This persuasion did not come from Him who called you.

9 A little leaven leavens the whole lump.

10 I have confidence toward you in the Lord, that you will reject this other persuasion, but the one that troubles you will bear his judgment, whoever he is.

11 However, if I still preach circumcision, why am I still persecuted? Then the stumbling block of the cross has been removed.

12 I would that those who disturb you would even go beyond circumcision and emasculate themselves.

Using Freedom to Love

13 For you, brethren, were called to freedom; only do not use your freedom as an opportunity for the flesh, but through love to serve one another.

14 For the whole law is fulfilled in one word, even in this: **"You shall love your neighbor as yourself"** (see Leviticus 19:18).

15 If you bite and devour one another, take heed that you are not consumed by one of another.

16 I say, walk by the Spirit, and you will not fulfill the lust of the flesh.

17 For the lust of the flesh is contrary to the Spirit, and the Spirit is contrary to the flesh, because; these are contrary to one another so that you may not do the things that you would.

18 If you are led by the Spirit you are not under the law.

The Works of the Flesh

19 Now the works of the flesh are manifest, which are: fornication, impurity, lasciviousness,

20 idolatry, sorcery, enmities, strife, jealousies, wraths, factions, divisions, and separation into parties,

21 envying, drunkenness, mocking, and such things, of which I forewarn you, even as I did forewarn you, that those who practice such things will not inherit the kingdom of God.

The Fruit of the Spirit

22 The fruit of the Spirit is love, joy, peace, patience, kindness, goodness, faithfulness,

23 meekness, self-control; against such there is no law.

24 Those who belong to Christ Jesus have crucified the flesh with the passions and the lusts thereof.

25 If we live by the Spirit, let us also walk by the Spirit.

26 Let us not become arrogant, provoking one another, envying one another.

Legalism Severs from Christ

Galatians 5:1-12: In the most sobering and direct statement made about the deception of turning to the law for righteousness, Paul makes it clear that when we do this, it severs us from Christ and the righteousness imputed by His cross for our salvation. It is obvious and logical that these two cannot co-exist. Either we receive His righteousness, or we try to establish our own by keeping the law. We cannot have it both ways.

Those whom Paul is addressing about receiving circumcision were adults who were receiving it for the purpose of complying with the law, as he makes clear that "every man that receives circumcision" (5:3). Many have their sons circumcised for health reasons. This is not what Paul is talking about here.

Using Freedom to Love

5:13-18: Being freed from the bondage of the law does not mean that we can do anything and be forgiven. Rather, we have the higher obligation to walk by the Spirit and to use our freedom for love. Freedom from the law is to walk by the Spirit. The Spirit would never lead us to do anything that is contrary to the righteous standards of God.

The Works of the Flesh

5:19-21: This is the clearest statement in Scripture identifying the works of the carnal nature. As Paul states, if we "practice" such things, we will not inherit the kingdom of God. This is not to imply that if we fall to one of these, we are doomed. Rather, if we practice them—give into them without fighting to overcome them—we will forfeit our inheritance in the kingdom. This should compel us to wage war against this nature as we are instructed here.

The Fruit of the Spirit

5:22-26: The way we war against the carnal nature is to walk by the Spirit. The fulfillment of walking by the Spirit is much greater than any satisfaction we could get from the carnal nature. This also starves the carnal nature, weakening it in our lives until we are dead to it.

NOTES

Paul's Letter to the
GALATIANS
Galatians 6

The Spiritual Restore

1 Brethren, if a man is caught in any transgression, you who are spiritual restore such a one, doing it in a spirit of gentleness considering yourself lest you also be tempted.

2 Bear one another's burdens, and so fulfill the law of Christ.

3 For if a man thinks himself to be something when he is not, he deceives himself.

4 Let each man prove his own work, and then he will have his glorying in regard to himself alone, and not because of his neighbor.

5 For each man will bear his own burden.

6 Let him who is taught the word share all good things with him that teaches.

Sowing and Reaping

7 Do not be deceived, God is not mocked, for whatever a man sows that will he also reap.

8 For he who sows to his own flesh will from the flesh reap corruption, but he who sows to the Spirit will from the Spirit reap eternal life.

9 Let us not grow weary in doing good, for in due season we will reap if we do not grow weary.

10 So then, as we have the opportunity let us do good to all men, and especially toward those who are of the household of faith.

11 Notice the large letters are that I write to you with my own hand.

12 As many as desire to make a show in the flesh compel you to be circumcised so that they may not be persecuted for the cross of Christ.

13 For not even those who receive circumcision keep the law themselves, but they desire to have you circumcised so that they may glory in your flesh.

The New Creation

14 Far be it from me to glory except in the cross of our Lord Jesus Christ, through which the world has been crucified to me, and I was crucified to the world.

15 For neither is circumcision anything, nor un-circumcision, but *what matters is the* new creation.

16 As many as will walk by this rule, peace be upon them, and mercy, and upon the Israel of God.

17 From now on let no man trouble me; for I have branded on my body the marks of Jesus.

18 The grace of our Lord Jesus Christ be with your spirit, brethren. Amen.

The Spiritual Restore

Galatians 6:1-6: Those who are spiritual will be devoted to restoring the fallen, not condemning them. When man fell, the Lord did not condemn us, but came and laid down His life for us. His true followers will do the same for others. However, this does not mean that we just overlook sin. We must confront it when it arises in the church, just as we see in the example of this great apostle. Even so, we do this for the purpose of redemption in a spirit of gentleness, knowing if we become arrogant, we can fall to the same things.

Sowing and Reaping

6:7-13: As sure as the law of gravity is a natural law, the fact that we will reap what we sow is a spiritual law that is certain. For this reason, we should always consider what we are sowing with our words and our behavior. If we sow division or strife, we can be sure it will come back on us. If we sow peace and reconciliation that is according to the Spirit of Christ, then this is what we will reap. If we sow to the carnal nature, it will grow. If we sow to the Spirit, then we will grow strong in Spirit.

The New Creation

6:14-18: The conclusion of the whole matter is to walk in the power of the new creation. We must not walk in the flesh or turn to the law, instead we must abide in the grace of the Lord Jesus. It is that simple. We must never allow ourselves to be beguiled from this simplicity of devotion to Christ.

Summation

This letter to the Galatians stands as the most clear and powerful truth in the New Testament to confront legalism. It was written by one who was the "Pharisee of Pharisees" and is, therefore, one of the most extraordinary demonstrations of the power of God's grace through the New Covenant.

The young, first-century church came under a relentless attack by those who sought to impose the Law of Moses upon her. This attack has not abated throughout the centuries. It now comes in many forms, not just through those seeking to impose the Law of Moses upon her (though this is still happening too). This is because the enemy of our souls knows very well that this is the primary way to cause believers to sever themselves from Christ and the power of the cross—that which has defeated him. Because of the power of Paul's writings against this, legalists today must attack Paul and his credibility as an apostle.

It was legalists who constantly challenged Jesus as He walked the earth. They were the ones who had Him crucified. There are many legalists who have been sown as tares throughout the body of Christ. We are told they will be removed before the end, but now they are allowed to test believers in their faith and devotion to the truth. Fundamental to walking with Christ in the power of the New Covenant is walking in the liberty of the Spirit. We must resist legalism at every point, just as this great apostle did.

Even so, there is a ditch on either side of the path of life. Legalism is on one side and lawlessness is on the other. Those who fall into one ditch often overreact and fall into the ditch on the other side. We must learn to walk between the extremes of lawlessness and legalism if we are going to stay on the path of life.

NOTES

Paul's Letter to The Galatians Proper Names and Definitions

Abba: father

Abraham: father of a great multitude, exalted father

Antioch: speedy as a chariot

Arabia: evening, desert, ravens, wilderness

Barnabas: son of the prophet, or of consolation

Cephas: a rock or stone

Christ: anointed

Cilici: which rolls or overturns

Damascus: a sack full of blood, the similitude of burning, city of Syria, silent is the sackcloth weaver

Galatia: white, the color of milk

Gentiles: the nations or pagan

Hagar: a stranger, one that fears, ensnaring

Isaac: laughter, he shall laugh, mockery

Israel: who prevails with God, he shall be prince of God

James: that supplants, undermines, heel-catcher, he whom God protects

Jerusalem: vision of peace, foundation of peace, restoring or teaching of peace

Jesus: Savior, Deliverer, Yahweh is salvation

Jew: the praise of the Lord, confession

John: the grace or mercy of the Lord

Judaea: the praise of the Lord, confession

Paul: small, little

Peter: a rock or stone

Sinai: a bush, enmity, thorny

Syria: Aram, exalted, high tableland

Titus: pleasing

INTRODUCTION
PAUL'S LETTER TO THE EPHESIANS

This letter is heralded by some as not only the greatest writing in the New Testament, but the greatest writing of all time. The reason for this is that it covers a variety of themes with unusual depth, clarity, power, and economy of words. If one had to choose only one book of The Bible to read for the rest of their life, Ephesians would have to be a high consideration.

For the way that it seamlessly combines lofty vision with practical application, Ephesians is possibly without peer. It is the only book in The Bible for which I have written a verse-by-verse commentary. This is because every verse is so full of important insight that it compels you to stop and ponder. Many writers throughout the age have attempted to express the same themes in large and even multiple volumes without accomplishing what Paul does in this one short letter. It is a literary marvel as well as a spiritual one.

As the main precept of Colossians is to establish the centrality and purpose of Christ, the main theme of Ephesians is to establish the place and purpose of the church. By no means is this to imply that the revelation of the church is more important than the revelation of Christ. However, this understanding of the church is built upon Christ and His cause and how He so deserves a worthy bride. Then the apostle lays out how the church will become what she is called to be.

Most scholars tend to agree that this letter was likely penned by Paul during his imprisonment in Rome about A.D.60 or 61. As is Paul's custom in all of his letters, he begins with a brief but powerful presentation of the basic gospel and our redemption through Christ. Then he establishes the place of Christ as the ultimate purpose of God, concluding with the remarkable statement that all creation will ultimately be summed up in Him. This is the ultimate purpose of God that we must stay focused upon, or we will be distracted by the lesser purposes. This is the foundation that all of Paul's writings and works are built upon, as is the case with every true apostolic ministry.

Upon this foundation, the greatest of all the purposes of creation has been given to the church. She is not just called to be His force in the world, His body, but she is called to be united with Him, to be His bride, His joint heir, His temple and dwelling place. It is noteworthy that this is written to the Ephesian church that lived in the shadow of the temple to the Greek goddess Diana, the antithesis of all that the church is called to be.

The centrality of Christ is the basic theme of The Bible. It is the core theme from Genesis to Revelation, yet nowhere is the purpose of the church stated with such clarity and power as in Ephesians. Even so, the only way the church can come into her full purpose is to grow up in all things into Christ, keeping her focus on Him and the things above where He is seated. Indeed, the church will never become what she is called to be by focusing on herself. She must know who she is and what she is called to do. However, the way of attaining this is by knowing who He is and what He has already attained.

The church's highest purpose is to contain within herself the fullness of Christ—to be His body and the extension of Him—doing His will as He continues to do His work on the earth through His body. Our goal must always be to reveal Him, not ourselves. It is to reveal Him that the church is given His power and authority. She does this from a position of being seated with Him on His throne.

The church is the temple of the Lord. We are His habitation, His dwelling place. If God is in His temple, the temple will not get the attention, regardless of how wonderful it is. If we are the focus of people's attention, we must wonder if He is indeed dwelling in us. The Lord will bless many things He will not inhabit. An ultimate question to ask is whether we have the *blessing* of the Lord, but not Him.

After so powerfully articulating this great purpose of the church to contain the fullness of Christ, Paul lays out the practical plan for achieving it. He begins by listing and explaining the gift ministries that have been given to the church for raising her up into what she is called to be. Then he describes the character and attitudes required for this diverse body to function in the unity necessary. It is not just the unity of a common doctrine, but the unity of a common life in the Spirit that will ultimately result in a community like no other the world has ever seen. This cannot be accomplished just by the resolutions of men. It is a grace from above.

To fortify this high purpose of the church, the apostle gives practical instructions for the family, husbands and wives, and the raising of children. The family is the basic relationship God gave, which is to be a reflection of His relationship to His family. Strengthening the family is, therefore, primary to strengthening the church. The behavior of believers must be above reproach. As the Lord came to lay down His life for us, we are required to do the same for others. The church is called to be a living demonstration of God's love for mankind and the earth.

The apostle warns of the enemy's intent to thwart this great purpose of the church, just as he sought to destroy Christ. A main strategy of the devil is to destroy our unity. Paul gives a simple but effective strategy for defending against this evil intent.

The apostle concludes this brilliant letter by again encouraging the saints to live in a manner worthy of their calling, behaving always in such a way as to glorify the Lord, and, having put on their armor, continuing in prayer. The church's calling to be the ultimate royalty in all of creation is a position of intercession for all of creation. As the greatest in His kingdom will always be the greatest servants, the church will be great because of her common devotion to this.

Paul's Letter to the Ephesians

Ephesians 1

Salutation

1 Paul, by the will of God an apostle of Christ Jesus, to the saints who are at Ephesus, and the faithful in Christ Jesus:

2 Grace to you, and peace from God our Father and the Lord Jesus Christ.

3 Blessed be the God and Father of our Lord Jesus Christ, who has blessed us with every spiritual blessing in the heavenly places, in Christ.

Called Before the World Began

4 He chose us in Him before the foundation of the world, so that we should be holy and without blemish, before Him in love.

5 He has predestined us for adoption as His own sons through Jesus Christ, according to the good pleasure of His will.

6 This is to the praise of the glory of His grace, which He freely bestowed on us in the Beloved.

7 In Him we have our redemption through His blood, the forgiveness of our trespasses, according to the riches of His grace,

8 which he made to abound toward us through all wisdom and understanding.

The Mystery of His Will

9 He made known to us the mystery of His will, according to His good pleasure that He purposed in Him,

10 until the fullness of times when all things will be summed up in Christ, the things in the heavens, and the things upon the earth, in Him.

11 It is in Him that we were also made to be an inheritance, having been predestined according to the purpose of Him who works all things after the counsel of His will.

12 It is for this purpose that we should be to the praise of His glory, we who had before hoped in Christ,

13 in whom you also, having heard the word of truth, the gospel of your salvation, having also believed, you were sealed with the Holy Spirit of promise.

14 This is a down payment of our inheritance, the redemption of God's own possession, to the praise of His glory.

15 For this cause I also, having heard of the faith in the Lord Jesus which is among you, and the love which you show toward all the saints,

16 do not cease to give thanks for you, making mention of you in my prayers.

Eyes to See

17 I ask that the God of our Lord Jesus Christ, the Father of glory, may give to you a spirit of wisdom and revelation in the knowledge of Him,

18 so that you would have the eyes of your heart opened, so that you may know what the hope of His calling is, what are the riches of the glory of His inheritance in the saints,

19 and the exceeding greatness of His power toward us who believe, that is according to the working of the strength of His might.

His Place in Heaven and in Us

20 This was wrought through Christ, when He raised Him from the dead, and made Him to sit at His right hand in the heavenly places,

21 far above all rule, and authority, and power, and dominion, and every name that is named, not only in this age, but also in that which is to come,

22 in which He will put all things in subjection under His feet, having given Him to be Head over all things to the church,

23 which is His body, the fullness of Him that fills all things.

Salutation

Ephesians 1:1-3: Paul's standard greeting is a blessing of grace and peace followed by encouragement about the calling and destiny of believers. He reminds them of their spiritual blessings in the heavenly places because this is a reality every believer must be fortified in. This was Paul's letter to the Ephesians, but it is God's letter to us. We should receive the same things as a personal reminder from the Lord.

Called Before the World Began

1:4-8: We were all known before the foundation of the world in the Lord's heart when He brought forth the creation. He also has a specific purpose and destiny that should be a basic devotion of every Christian to know and fulfill.

The Mystery of His Will

1:9-16: The apostle points to the reason for their calling and the reason for all creation—that everything in heaven and earth will ultimately be summed up in Christ. This is the ultimate purpose of all things and is our ultimate purpose as well. Everything in our lives is allowed for the purpose of helping to conform us into the image of the Son. This is the ultimate purpose of God. If we do not keep our attention on the ultimate purpose of God, we will be continually distracted by the lesser purposes of God. If we keep our attention on this ultimate purpose, we can quickly and easily understand everything that is happening in our lives—it is all meant to conform us to the image of Christ.

Eyes to See

1:17-19: When the eyes of our hearts are opened, which are our spiritual eyes, we see the greatness of His power toward us. Our goal should be to see more clearly with these spiritual eyes than we do with our natural eyes. When we do this, we will live by a different reality.

His Place in Heaven and in Us

1:20-23: Now our attention is again turned to Christ and His elevated place in creation. In His ultimate victory, we have the ultimate victory. Knowing and living by the truth of this one chapter would result in a life that would have major impact in this world and help to prepare it for the kingdom that is surely coming.

NOTES

Paul's Letter to the Ephesians

Ephesians 2

Our Resurrection

1 You He made alive, even when you were dead because of your trespasses and sins,

2 in which you once walked according to the course of this age, according to the prince of the powers of the air, the spirit that now works in the sons of disobedience;

3 in whom we also all once lived in the lust of our flesh, fulfilling the desires of the flesh, and of the mind, and were by nature children of wrath, even as the rest.

4 However, God, being rich in mercy, for His great love with which He loved us,

5 even when we were dead because of our trespasses, He made us alive together with Christ. By grace have you been saved!

6 He also raised us up with Him, and made us to sit with Him in the heavenly places, in Christ Jesus,

7 so that in the ages to come He might show the exceeding riches of His grace in kindness toward us in Christ Jesus.

8 For by grace have you been saved through faith, and that not of yourselves, it is the gift of God.

9 It is not of works, so that no man should become arrogant.

10 For we are His workmanship, created in Christ Jesus for good works, which God prepared before that we should walk in them.

11 Therefore remember that once you, the Gentiles according to the flesh, who are called un-circumcision by that which is called the circumcision, which is in the flesh, made by hands,

12 so that you were at that time separate from Christ, alienated from the commonwealth of Israel, and strangers from the covenants of the promise, having no hope and without God in the world,

13 but now in Christ Jesus you who were once far from God are brought close through the blood of Christ.

Our Unity in Him

14 For He is our peace, Who made both into one, and broke down the dividing wall *between the Jews and Gentiles*,

15 having abolished the enmity in His flesh, even the law of commandments contained in ordinances, so that He might create in Himself from the two one new man, making peace between them,

16 and so that He might reconcile them both in one body to God through the cross, having slain the enmity by it.

17 He came and preached **"peace to you that were far off, and peace to those who were close"** (see Isaiah 57:19).

18 For it is through Him that we both have our access in one Spirit to the Father.

The House of God

19 So then you are no longer strangers and sojourners, but you are fellow-citizens with the saints, and of the household of God,

20 being built upon the foundation of the apostles and prophets, Christ Jesus Himself being the chief Cornerstone.

21 It is in Him that each are being built up, fitly framed together, and are growing into a holy temple in the Lord.

22 It is in Him whom you are built together for a habitation of God in the Spirit.

Our Resurrection

Ephesians 2:1-13: We were already dead in sin and now are alive in Christ. This is a form of resurrection and the beginning of our resurrection. Even so, the great and sure hope of Christianity is the resurrection from the dead to our eternal reward. The resurrection from our "body of death" is eternal. With our heavenly body, we will live more wonderfully than we could ever imagine in this life. Our deliverance from sin is the down payment, the first fruits, of our resurrection to eternal life, and this life should also reflect the glorious one to come.

Our Unity in Him

2:14-18: The unity between Jew and Gentile is an earthly manifestation of the gospel applied. This is the breaking down of the ultimate racial barrier. Once it is overcome, the true peace of God will be manifested through His people on the earth.

The House of God

2:19-22: When Paul says "so then," it indicates that this will be the result of the barrier between Jew and Gentile being done away with—God will have a place to dwell among men by His Spirit.

In verse 20, we are told that the church has been built upon the foundation laid by the apostles and prophets. Some take this literally, that every congregation should have its foundation laid by the ministry of an apostle and prophet. This could be true, but also the foundation of the entire church was laid by the apostles and prophets.

This foundation began with our relationship to Jesus Christ. Then the bonding together of believers in *koinonia* fellowship was begun. Lastly, the *ecclesia* organization of the church and its government was given. It is crucial that we keep the building of churches in this order as well: Christ first and growing up into the Head is the basis of all things, and then our bonding together as a family must be before organization. We need organization and leadership, but if we become an organization more than a family, we are no longer the church that He designed.

NOTES

Paul's Letter to the Ephesians
Ephesians 3

The Great Mystery

1 For this cause, I Paul, the prisoner of Christ Jesus on behalf of you Gentiles,

2 as you have heard of the dispensation of that grace of God that was given to me toward you,

3 how that by revelation it was made known to me the mystery, as I wrote before briefly,

4 so that when you read you can perceive my understanding into the mystery of Christ.

5 In other generations this was not made known to the sons of men, as it has now been revealed to His holy apostles and prophets in the Spirit.

6 That is, that the Gentiles are fellow-heirs and fellow-members of the body, and fellow-partakers of the promise in Christ Jesus through the gospel.

7 For this gospel I was made a minister, according to the gift of the grace of God that was given to me according to the working of His power.

The Least of The Saints

8 To me, who is the least of all saints, was this grace given, to preach to the Gentiles the unsearchable riches of Christ,

9 and to make all men see what is the dispensation of the mystery which for ages has been hidden in God who created all things,

10 with the intent that now even to the principalities and the powers in the heavenly places it might be made known through the church, this manifold wisdom of God.

11 This is according to the eternal purpose that he purposed in Christ Jesus our Lord,

12 in whom we have boldness and confident access through our faith in Him.

13 Therefore I ask that you not faint because of my tribulations on your behalf, which are your glory.

14 For this cause I bow my knees to the Father,

15 from whom every family in heaven and on earth is named.

Power to Walk in His Fullness

16 *I pray* that He would grant to you, according to the riches of His glory, to be strengthened with power through His Spirit in the inner man,

17 so that Christ may dwell in your hearts through faith, and the result being that you are being rooted and grounded in love,

18 and may be strong enough to apprehend with all the saints what is the breadth and length and height and depth,

19 and to know the love of Christ that passes knowledge, that you may be filled with all the fullness of God.

20 Now to Him that is able to do exceeding abundantly above all that we ask or think, according to the power that works in us,

21 to Him be the glory in the church, and in Christ Jesus to all generations for ever and ever. Amen.

The Great Mystery

Ephesians 3:1-7: Paul calls the gospel "the mystery of Christ." From the beginning, it has been God's ultimate intent to restore everything that was lost by the Fall. The gospel of redemption, salvation, and reconciliation to God was always intended for the whole world. The Jews had a special place as

custodians of the Word of God and His revelation of redemption until it could be made known to the world through Christ. However, this was not God's only purpose for the gospel. He is also calling out from among fallen men those who would love Him, serve Him, and lay down their lives for Him daily so they could be found worthy to become members of His own household, joint heirs with Christ, the sons and daughters of God.

The Least of The Saints

3:8-15: This letter was written near the end of Paul's life, yet he still could not talk about the greatness of the calling we have in Christ without being enraptured by it. God emptying Himself and becoming a man and then, as a man, suffering all that He did for our sake, even fallen mankind, will be a marvel forever.

Paul concludes with the thought that every family on earth is descended from God, who has given life to all. Therefore, He will redeem those from every nation who will receive His grace.

In the sequence of Paul's letters, he goes from first calling himself "not inferior to the most eminent apostles" to "the least of the apostles" to what he says here, that he is "the least of the saints." In one of his last writings, he refers to himself as "the greatest of sinners." Here we see the pattern of true spiritual maturity. Because of the truth that "God resists the proud, but gives His grace to the humble," with true spiritual maturity and authority, there will be increasing humility.

Power to Walk in His Fullness

3:16-21: The way to be strengthened in our inner man and for Christ to dwell in our hearts is through knowing His love. Knowledge is important, but love surpasses knowledge.

NOTES

Paul's Letter to the Ephesians
Ephesians 4

To Walk in a Worthy Manner

1 I therefore, the prisoner in the Lord, beseech you to walk in a manner worthy of the calling with which you were called,

2 with all humility and meekness, with patience, bearing with one another in love,

3 giving diligence to keep the unity of the Spirit in the bond of peace.

4 There is one body and one Spirit, even as you also were called in one hope of your calling.

5 There is one Lord, one faith, one baptism,

6 one God and Father of all, who is over all, and through all, and in all.

7 To each one of us was the grace given according to the measure of the gift of Christ.

8 Therefore He says, **"When he ascended on high, he led captivity captive, and gave gifts to men"** (see Psalm 68:18).

9 Now this saying, that "He ascended," what does it mean except that He also descended into the lower parts of the earth?

10 He that descended is the same also that ascended far above all the heavens that He might fill all things.

His Continuing Ministry

11 He gave some to be apostles, and some prophets, and some evangelists, and some pastors, and teachers;

12 for the equipping of the saints to do the work of the ministry, to the building up of the body of Christ,

13 until we all attain to the unity of the faith, to the knowledge of the Son of God, to a mature man, to the measure of the stature that belongs to the fullness of Christ,

14 so that we may no longer be like children, tossed back and forth, and carried about with every wind of doctrine, by the trickery of men, who in craftiness use deceitful schemes.

15 Speaking the truth in love, we are to grow up in all things into Him, who is the Head, even Christ,

16 through Whom the whole body is fitted and held together through that which every joint supplies, according to the proper working of each individual part, makes for the increase and building up of the body in love.

From Old to New

17 This I say therefore, and testify in the Lord, that you no longer walk as the Gentiles walk, in the vanity of their mind,

18 being darkened in their understanding, alienated from the life of God because of the ignorance that is in them, because of the hardening of their heart.

19 These have lost their sensitivity, and given themselves up to lasciviousness, to work all uncleanness with greediness.

20 You did not learn about Christ in this way,

21 if it is true that you have heard Him, and were taught by Him, even as truth is in Jesus.

22 Now you put away that which concerns your former manner of life, the old man that is corrupted by lusts and deceit,

23 and that you be renewed in the spirit of your mind,

24 and put on the new man, which in the likeness of God has been created in righteousness, and holiness, and truth.

25 Therefore, putting away falsehood, speak truth each one of you with his neighbor—for we are members one of another.

26 Do not be given to anger, as this will cause you to sin. For this reason do not let the sun go down on your wrath,

27 and you will not give place to the devil.

28 Let him that stole steal no more, but rather let him labor, working with his hands for that which is good, that he may have an something to give to him that has need.

How Not to Grieve the Spirit

29 Let no unrighteous words proceed from your mouth, but only such as are good for the edification of others, according to the need of the moment, that they may give grace to those who hear.

30 Do not grieve the Holy Spirit of God, in whom you were sealed until the day of redemption,

31 letting all bitterness, and wrath, and anger, and clamor, and slander, be put away from you, along with all malice.

32 and be kind one to another, tenderhearted, forgiving each other, even as God also in Christ forgave you.

To Walk in a Worthy Manner

Ephesians 4:1-10: After the description of our high calling in Christ in the previous chapter, the obvious consequence of this knowledge should be for us to walk in a manner worthy of that calling. This is described as walking in love and unity. Such a walk is evidence that one has had the revelation of their purpose in Christ. Then we comprehend that He has given to us the gifts of the Spirit, the same ones He used when walking the earth, so that we might walk the same way. He continues to use His body, the church, to do His works. His ultimate purpose is to fill us with Himself, then "fill all things," which were created by Him, through Him, and for Him.

His Continuing Ministry

4:11-16: The failure of church leadership to comply with this crucial text to "equip the saints to do the work of the ministry"

is a root of the church's basic failure to be what it is called to be. When this text becomes the emphasis in the church that it deserves to be, the accomplishment of what the church is called to be is near. It will take these five equipping ministries, who equip the saints, to build up the body so that every part of the body is working before we can grow up in all things into Christ as we are called.

Because we cannot yet point to a church in the earth that has attained to the stature of Christ, and these ministries were all given "until" we attain to this stature, we know that all of these ministries are still needed and are, therefore, still found in the earth. Even so, the true ones are rare because so few are fulfilling this basic purpose of equipping others. We expect seminaries or other schools to do what every ministry is called to do if they are, in fact, one of these listed in verse 11.

As Paul writes, one of the primary reasons why so many believers are still blown about by every wind of doctrine is the failure of leadership to equip members of the body to know and function in their ministry.

From Old to New

4:17-28: Those who have been born of God are a new creation. If we have been renewed, our life should reflect it in godly behavior that is founded on truth and integrity. Above all, our lives should manifest the love of God.

How Not to Grieve the Spirit

4:29-32: What grieves the Spirit is our poor treatment of one another. If we love God, we will love His people and treat them in the same way that we would treat Him. He explained this in The Parable of the Sheep and Goats.

NOTES

Paul's Letter to the
EPHESIANS
Ephesians 5

Be Imitators of God

1 Therefore be imitators of God, as beloved children;

2 and walk in love, even as Christ also loved you, and gave Himself up for us, an offering and a sacrifice to God for a sweet smelling aroma.

3 Let not fornication, any form of impurity, or greed, even be named among you, as is becoming of the saints.

4 Nor vulgar or foolish talk, or vulgar jesting, which are not befitting, but rather *be devoted to the* giving of thanks.

These Will Not Inherit the Kingdom

5 For this you know for sure, that no fornicator, nor unclean person, nor covetous man, who is an idolater, has any inheritance in the kingdom of Christ and God.

6 Let no man deceive you with empty words, for it is because of these things that the wrath of God will come upon the sons of disobedience.

7 Therefore do not be partakers with them.

8 For you were once in darkness, but are now in the light in the Lord.

9 Walk as children of light, which is to walk in the fruit of the light, in all goodness and righteousness and truth.

10 Prove what is pleasing to the Lord,

11 and have no fellowship with the unfruitful works of darkness, but rather reprove them.

12 It is a shame even to speak of the things that are done by them in secret.

13 All things when they are proven are made manifest by the light, for everything that is made manifest is light.

14 Therefore He says, **"Awake, you that sleep, and arise from the dead, and Christ will shine upon you"** (see Isaiah 26:19, 60:1-2).

15 Therefore watch carefully how you walk, not as the unwise, but as wise,

16 redeeming the time because the days are evil.

17 Therefore do not be foolish, but understand what the will of the Lord is.

18 Do not be drunk with wine, which is dissipation and excess, but be filled and satisfied with the Spirit.

19 Speak to one another in psalms and hymns and spiritual songs, singing and making melody with your heart to the Lord,

20 giving thanks always for all things in the name of our Lord Jesus Christ to God, even the Father,

21 subjecting yourselves to one another in the fear of Christ.

Instruction for Wives

22 Wives, respect and be devoted to your own husbands as unto the Lord.

23 For the husband is the head of the wife just as Christ is the Head of the church, being Himself the Savior of the body.

24 Just as the church is subject to Christ, so let the wives also be to their husbands in everything.

Instruction for Husbands

25 Husbands, love your wives, even as Christ also loved the church, and gave Himself up for it,

26 so that He might sanctify it, having cleansed it by the washing of water with the word,

27 so that He might present the church to Himself in glory, not having either spot or wrinkle, or any such thing, but that it should be holy and without blemish.

28 Even as this, husbands love their own wives as their own bodies. He that loves his own wife loves himself,

29 because no man ever hated his own flesh, but nourishes and cherishes it, even as Christ does the church,

30 because we are members of His body.

31 **"For this reason a man will leave his father and mother, and will cleave to his wife; and the two will become one flesh"** (see Genesis 2:24).

32 This mystery is great, but I speak in regard to Christ and the church.

33 Nevertheless, let each of you love his own wife even as himself; and let the wife see that she respects her husband.

Be Imitators of God

Ephesians 5:1-4: We are called to be like Jesus and do the works He did. This is how we do it: we begin with love. Love compels us to walk in purity with our spirit, soul, and body. Something can be legal but still not be right. If we have a question about whether something is appropriate for a son or daughter of the King, we should consider if it is something we think Jesus would do.

These Will Not Inherit the Kingdom

5:5-21: This is the basic code of behavior for the holy and royal sons and daughters of God. As is clear here and in other Scriptures, those who practice deeds of darkness will not inherit the kingdom of God. This does not mean that someone who falls and then repents is excluded, but rather those who give themselves to sin and continue in it as a practice.

To know and walk in the will of the Lord is the counter and antidote to the sin that is seeking to destroy us. As we see in Romans 12:1-2, when we are "living sacrifices" as we are called to be, and are not conformed to the world but rather transformed, then we can "prove what the will of the Lord is." Every Christian should be able to prove beyond a doubt what God's will is for their life. If we cannot do this, then, at the very least, we are living far below what we are called to. It is also likely that sin is getting a grip on us so that our love is becoming cold.

Instruction for Wives

5:22-24: This exhortation for wives to be subject to their husbands is consistent with the teachings and practices of Christians from the first century. However, nowhere does it say that women should be submitted to men. It is only in the family relationship that a wife is to be submitted to her husband as the head of the family, but this does not carry over into any other relationship of women to men.

Neither does this indicate that women are second-class citizens in the Lord or not capable of leadership. In the Lord "there is no male or female." The headship of the man is for the practical, earthly leadership of the home. Anything with more than one head is a monster, so there must be a head, but that does not mean that the wife has no input or authority.

The husband and wife are also called to the high purpose of revealing the relationship of Christ to His bride, the church. The greatest saints are those who have most fully submitted to Christ, obeying Him in all things. True submission is not bondage or oppression, rather it is one of the greatest demonstrations of faith. When true submission is seen, it is glorious. We also see throughout the New Testament the remarkable authority that the Lord has given to His church.

The Proverbs 31 woman is an example of godly, holy submission. She is loved and honored by her husband. Her life is a joy to him and brings great honor to him. She takes initiative and leadership in the affairs of the family, and this is greatly esteemed. In the Lord, the one in authority is to be the greatest servant. So by serving her in this way, the man frees his wife to use her gifts and callings to become all she is created to be. Therefore, she is like this woman who excels in all she puts her hands to.

Instruction for Husbands

5:25-33: This is how the practical demeanor of a Christian is brought home and is a foundation for the family. Love is the foundation of all true spiritual authority. When our leadership is guided by love, then it will be the kind that all will want to live under.

NOTES

Paul's Letter to the
EPHESIANS
Ephesians 6

Instructions for Behavior

1 Children, obey your parents in the Lord, for this is right.

2 Honor your father and mother which is the first commandment with promise (see Exodus 20:12; Deuteronomy 5:26),

3 so that it may go well with you, and you may live long on the earth.

4 Fathers, do not provoke your children to wrath, but nurture them with the chastening and admonition of the Lord.

5 Servants, be obedient to those who are your masters according to the flesh with fear and trembling, with devotion serving as if doing it for Christ.

6 Do not do this just for appearances, as men-pleasers, but as servants of Christ, doing the will of God from the heart.

7 Serve with a good attitude as unto the Lord, not just for men.

8 Know that whatever good thing each one does, the same will he receive again from the Lord, whether he is bond or free.

9 Masters, do the same thing to those who serve you, not being overbearing, or threatening, knowing that He who is both their Master and yours is in heaven, and there is no respect of persons with Him.

Our Struggle

10 Finally, be strong in the Lord and in the strength of His might.

11 Put on the whole armor of God so that you may be able to stand against the wiles of the devil.

12 We do not wrestle with flesh and blood, but against the principalities, against the powers, against the world-rulers of this darkness, against the spiritual armies of wickedness in the heavenly places.

Our Armor

13 Therefore take up the whole armor of God so that you may be able to stand in the evil day, and, having done all, to stand.

14 Stand therefore, having girded your loins with truth, and having put on the breastplate of righteousness.

15 Have your feet shod with the preparation of the gospel of peace (see Isaiah 52:7).

16 Always holding up the shield of faith with which you will be able to quench all the fiery darts of the evil one.

17 Finally, take the helmet of salvation, and the sword of the Spirit, which is the word of God.

The Focus of Prayer

18 Pray about all things, and pray at all times in the Spirit. Watch with perseverance, and pray for all the saints.

19 Pray on my behalf, that utterance may be given to me when I open my mouth to make known with boldness the mystery of the gospel,

20 for which I am an ambassador in chains. Pray that in this I may speak boldly as I ought to speak.

21 So that you also may know my affairs, and how I am doing, Tychicus, the beloved brother and faithful minister in the Lord, will make known to you all things.

22 I have sent him to you for this very purpose, that you may know our condition, and that he may comfort your hearts.

23 Peace be to the brethren, and love with faith from God the Father and the Lord Jesus Christ.

24 Grace be with all who love our Lord Jesus Christ with a love that is not corruptible.

Instructions for Behavior

Ephesians 6:1-9: Honoring our fathers and mothers has the promise from God that it will go well with us, and we will live long on the earth. He does not say honor just great parents, or even good ones, but the ones we were given. Finding a way to honor our parents can be one of the widest open doors for the blessings and favor of God in our lives.

Even a slave can be free if they live to serve Christ and do all they do as unto the Lord. There is no greater freedom we can ever know than to be Christ's slave. When we lay down our lives for Him, we find true life. When we seek to save our lives just to serve ourselves, we lose true life.

In modern terminology, this exhortation might be translated for workers to obey their supervisors, doing their work as unto the Lord not just as unto men. We should use our jobs, and all other relationships, as opportunities to serve Christ, because as we do unto even the least of His little ones, we are doing it as unto Him.

Our Struggle

6:10-12: Understanding the spiritual nature of our struggle compels us to know that we cannot fight in our own strength. We must seek the strength of the Lord. When we understand that we are not in conflict with people, but rather spiritual powers that use people, then we should be able to give more grace to people. Our victory is when those who oppose us are not beaten, but rather set free.

We must "wrestle" with principalities and powers. You can cast out demons, but you must wrestle with the higher powers. Wrestling is the closest form of combat. This is why Christians and churches are often attacked by the ruling evil powers in a region. Prayer alone will not end this. God uses the conflict to strengthen us in the opposite spirit and to ultimately cast out

the darkness by the light we walk in. For this reason, we must view every attack and conflict as an opportunity to grow in the Lord and in the use of the divinely powerful weapons we have been given—love and truth.

Our Armor

6:13-17: Now knowing the nature of our warfare, we need to know the nature of our armor, which is also spiritual. Each piece of armor has a different function that the mature Christian must be proficient at using.

The Focus of Prayer

6:18-24: Prayer is both a defensive and offensive weapon in our warfare. Paul asks the Ephesians to pray that he might have the boldness to preach the gospel as he should. Boldness is a basic characteristic that all of God's messengers should have.

Paul finishes his letter with his blessing of the grace and peace of the Lord. These are the most valuable things anyone could possess.

The church at Ephesus was one of the important first century churches. This letter to the Ephesians is one of the important letters of the New Testament. It is practical, addressing a broad spectrum of issues, yet with concise counsel. This letter contains the most comprehensive revelation of what the church is called to be and a standard by which we can measure our progress in maturity.

NOTES

Paul's Letter to The Ephesians Proper Names and Definitions

Christ: anointed

Ephesus: desirable

Gentiles: the nations or pagan

Israel: who prevails with God, he shall be prince of God

Jesus: Savior, Deliverer, Yahweh is salvation

Paul: small, little

Psalms: songs of praise

Tychicus: casual, by chance

INTRODUCTION
PAUL'S LETTER TO THE PHILIPPIANS

This Epistle was written by the Apostle Paul to the church he established at Philippi. This great church was birthed on his second missionary journey with Timothy and Silas, about A.D.50. Paul was prevented by the Lord from preaching the gospel in Asia (now Asia Minor). Then he was released by the Holy Spirit to go there through a dream he had of a Macedonian man asking for him to come and help them (see Acts 16:8-10). Paul and his team immediately set out to do so.

Philippi was a major Roman city with a proud heritage. It had Roman citizenship bestowed on it as a reward for battles it had fought for the Roman Empire. There was a Jewish community in the city, and the God-fearing women had a place of prayer outside of the city by a river. When Paul shared the gospel with these women, the favor of God was upon a merchant named Lydia from Thyatira. She became the first Christian convert from this region.

As was typical when Paul preached in a place of great spiritual destiny, a persecution rose up against Paul and his message immediately. The city officials had Paul and Silas arrested, beaten, thrown into the inner prison, and chained to the wall in stocks. As Paul and Silas were worshipping God in the night, an earthquake struck the city, opening the prison and releasing the prisoners from their chains. The jailer was about to kill himself, thinking that the prisoners had all escaped, but Paul stopped him saying that all of the prisoners were still there. When the jailer heard this, he opened his heart to the gospel and was granted salvation along with his family.

After the city officials granted release to Paul and Silas, they strengthened the new converts and then left for Thessalonica. There he preached the gospel and established another church with the new converts. Even though the new Christians at Philippi were very young in the faith, they showed great maturity and vision by sending provisions and support to Paul while he labored for the gospel in Thessalonica. Later they sent more resources for his support when he was in Corinth. This was very encouraging to Paul and to all who heard of it. Though this letter was mostly to thank the Philippians and commend them for their generosity, it includes one of the greatest discourses on the high calling of God in Christ to be found in the Scriptures. Paul obviously saw their maturity and vision for generosity as evidence of an uncommon grace to give themselves to this highest of all pursuits.

The Philippians also took up a large contribution for the saints in Jerusalem, which Paul personally carried to the apostles and elders there. With this, the church at Philippi became renowned among Christians everywhere for her faith and generosity—the foundational characteristics of those who are not just believing in grace, but walking in it.

NOTES

Paul's Letter to the
PHILIPPIANS
Philippians 1

Salutation

1 Paul and Timothy, servants of Christ Jesus, to all the saints in Christ Jesus that are at Philippi, along with the elders and deacons:

2 Grace to you and peace from God our Father and the Lord Jesus Christ.

3 I thank my God every time I think of you,

4 always making mention of you in my prayers, which I do with joy,

5 for your fellowship in the furtherance of the gospel from the first day until now.

The Great Hope

6 I am confident of this very thing, that He who began a good work in you will complete it, perfecting you for the day of Jesus Christ.

7 It is right for me to be convinced of this on behalf of you, because I have you in my heart, inasmuch as, both in my bonds and in the defense and confirmation of the gospel, you all are partakers with me of grace.

8 For God is my witness how I long after you in the tender mercies of Christ Jesus.

True Discernment

9 This is what I pray, that your love may abound more and more in true knowledge, and in all discernment.

10 This is so that you may approve the things that are excellent, that you may be sincere, and void of offence until the day of Christ,

11 being filled with the fruits of righteousness that we receive through Jesus Christ, to the glory and praise of God.

The Gospel Proclaimed

12 Now I would have you know, brethren, that the things that happened to me have resulted in the further progress of the gospel,

13 so that my bonds in Christ became known throughout the whole Praetorian Guard, and to all the rest.

14 And most of the brethren in the Lord became confident because of my imprisonment, and are now even bolder to speak the word of God without fear.

15 Some indeed preach Christ out of envy and strife, and some from good motives.

16 These do it out of love, knowing that I am appointed for the defense of the gospel,

17 but the others proclaim Christ to cause divisions, not in sincerity, thinking that they will cause me distress in my imprisonment.

18 What do I think? In every way, whether in pretense or in truth, I rejoice that Christ is proclaimed. Yes, I truly rejoice in this.

19 For I know that this will work toward my salvation, through your prayers, and the supply of the Spirit of Jesus Christ,

20 according to my earnest expectation and hope, and that in nothing will I be put to shame, but that with all boldness, as always, Christ will be magnified in my body, whether by life, or by death.

Choosing When to Depart This Life

21 For to me to live is Christ, and to die is gain.

22 But if to live in the flesh, if this will bring continued fruit from my work, then I do not know what I will choose.

23 I cannot decide between the two. I have the desire to depart and be with Christ, for that is very much better for me,

24 yet for me to continue to abide in the flesh is more needful for your sake.

25 I do have this confidence, I know that I will remain for a time to abide with you all, for your progress and joy in the faith,

26 so that your glorying may abound in Christ Jesus with me through my presence with you again.

A Life Worthy of The Gospel

27 Only let your manner of life be worthy of the gospel of Christ, so that, whether I come and see you, or remain absent, I may hear of your condition, that you stand fast in one spirit, with one soul striving for the faith of the gospel.

28 Do not in any way be disturbed by your adversaries, which is evidence of their perdition, but it is allowed by God for your salvation,

29 because for you it has been granted on behalf of Christ, not only to believe on Him, but also to suffer for His sake.

30 By this you are having the same conflict that you saw me go through, and now hear to be with me.

Salutation

1:1-5: As always, Paul's salutation is filled with encouragement and praise at their progress in the truth of the gospel. It is usually followed by correction, but Paul had nothing major to correct the Philippian church about. Their faith was so remarkable and mature that he began right away to discuss the foundational principles of the high calling of God in Christ Jesus, making this unique among the Pauline letters.

The Great Hope

1:6-8: The Lord does not start something He will not finish. Even so, the work is a joint effort between us and the Holy Spirit. That's why He is called "The Helper," not "The Doer." If it seems that our progress has stalled, it is often because He is waiting for us to join with Him or to do our part. The two ex-

tremes we often fall into are wanting Him to do it all or trying to do it all ourselves. We should always be aware of what the Lord is trying to work into our lives and be resolved to do our part. In all things be encouraged that He will not give up on us until the work is complete.

True Discernment

1:9-11: True discernment is founded on love, not suspicion. We cannot accurately discern another person or thing unless we love them. However, true love does not overlook sin or other failures, as this is much of what discernment is for, but true love addresses problems with a redemptive purpose instead of condemnation.

Paul also prayed that their love may abound in "true knowledge." Love is required for us to know anyone accurately.

The Gospel Proclaimed

1:12-20: The Lord is perfect, but He has chosen to proclaim His truth and do His work through imperfect vessels. If we had to be perfect for Him to use us, then no one could ever be used. He chooses to use some who can be so far from perfect and so immature in the faith, that it is a real stretch to see or acknowledge His work through them. This too is part of the gospel message—He loves us and will even use us while we are still a mess or immature. We are straightened out and grow into maturity by joining with Him in His work.

Consider this. Studies show that about 98% of those who come to the Lord do so through the witness of a friend or relative. About 98% of those are led to the Lord by a believer who has known the Lord only two years or less. New believers are the most powerful evangelistic force in the world. Why would we ever want to restrict them? And why is it that the "mature" cease to lead others to the Lord?

Many today preach Him with various motives, as Paul acknowledges. The Lord still uses this. Even so, let us not fall into the trap of thinking it is right to continue with wrong motives. We are called to grow up into Him. As we mature in Him, our motives should mature, too.

Choosing When to Depart This Life

1:21-26: Paul received the remarkable authority to choose when he would die and go be with the Lord. Obviously not all Christians have this, but it is available to all Christians. Just as Jesus laid down His own life, if we remain true to our discipleship to grow up in all things into Christ, we too can be given this authority.

A Life Worthy of The Gospel

1:27-30: Though the Lord may use those who preach out of pretense and various other motives, our goal should be that our lives reflect the character and nobility of the Lord and His truth. This character begins with unity with the rest of the body of Christ. This unity is based on the respect for the Lord's love of diversity and creativity.

All who call on His name are His children. Our regard for parents will be reflected in how we treat their children. For this reason, the way we treat the children of the Lord is a reflection of our regard for Him. Even when we must confront others concerning sin, error, or other problems, we must do so with respect and hope of redemption, not condemnation. The life that most reflects our God, who is Love, is demonstrated by love.

The apostle also states that the opposition and persecution they endure is for their salvation and is an indication that God has chosen them. When the apostles in Jerusalem were beaten for preaching the gospel, they went out rejoicing that they had been considered worthy to suffer shame for the sake of the name of the Lord. Persecution—to have all manner of evil spoken about us that is not true, physical attacks, imprisonment, and death—for preaching the gospel is one of the greatest honors that one can have. Just as Jesus still wears the marks of

His crucifixion, so will we keep the scars from our persecution as badges of honor for eternity.

NOTES

Paul's Letter to the
PHILIPPIANS
Philippians 2

Unity Through Christ

1 Therefore, if there is any exhortation in Christ, any consolation of love, any fellowship of the Spirit, if there are any tender mercies, or compassion,

2 make my joy complete, so that you are of the same devotion, having the same love, being of one accord, and of one mind.

3 Do nothing that would cause a faction, or with selfish ambition, but in humility of mind each of you count others as more important than yourself.

4 Do not look out just for your own interests, but also look out for the interests of others.

5 Have this mind in you that was in Christ Jesus.

6 He existed in the form of God, but did not count being equal with God a thing to be grasped,

7 but emptied Himself, taking the form of a servant being made in the likeness of men,

8 and being found in this fashion as a man, He humbled Himself, becoming obedient even unto death, even the death of the cross.

9 Therefore God highly exalted Him, and gave to Him the name that is above every name,

10 so that at the name of Jesus every knee will bow, of those in heaven, and those on the earth, and those under the earth,

11 and that every tongue will confess that Jesus Christ is Lord, to the glory of God the Father.

Working Out Our Salvation

12 So then, my beloved, even as you have always obeyed, not as in my presence only, but now much more in my absence, work out your own salvation with fear and trembling,

13 because it is God who works in you both to will and to work, for His good pleasure.

14 Do all things without complaining or questioning,

15 so that you may become blameless and harmless, children of God without blemish in the midst of a crooked and perverse generation, among whom you are seen as lights in the world.

16 Hold fast to the word of life so that I may have a reason to glory in the day of Christ, that I did not run in vain, neither labor in vain.

17 Yes, and if I am offered upon the sacrifice and service of your faith, I have joy, and rejoice with you all.

18 In the same manner you also have joy, and can rejoice with me.

Fellow Workers

19 But I hope in the Lord Jesus to send Timothy to you shortly, that I also may be comforted when I hear how you are doing.

20 For I have no one who is like-minded, who will truly care for your condition.

21 For the rest all seek their own interests, not the things of Jesus Christ.

22 But you know his character that as a child serves his father he served with me in furtherance of the gospel.

23 Therefore I hope to send him directly, as soon as I see how it will go with me,

24 and I trust in the Lord that I myself also will come shortly.

25 But I counted it necessary to send to you Epaphroditus, my brother and fellow worker, and fellow soldier, and your messenger and minister to my need,

26 as he longed after you all, and was very troubled, because you had heard that he was sick.

27 He was indeed sick and close to death, but God had mercy on him, and not only on him, but also on me, that I might not have sorrow upon sorrow.

28 Therefore I have sent him with even more diligence so that, when you see him again you may rejoice, and that I may be less sorrowful

29 Receive him therefore in the Lord with all joy, and hold such as him in honor,

30 because it was for the work of Christ that he came close to death, risking his life to supply that which was left behind in your service toward me.

Unity Through Christ

2:1-11: Spiritual maturity is reflected by the grace we have toward others, but ultimate maturity in Christ will be demonstrated by unity with the rest of the body of Christ. If we are properly related to the Head, we must also be properly related to His body, the church. Unity is not based on compromise, but on love and how the members of the body have taken on the nature of Christ to lay down their own lives for one another as unto the Lord. These reject selfish ambition and give themselves to the purposes of the Lord, and thereby, the purpose of building up His people and serving them.

Working Out Our Salvation

2:12-18: The "working out of our own salvation" that is addressed here is not the same as the salvation and eternal life we have received through the atonement of the cross. The salvation addressed here is the deliverance we go through in putting to death the old nature and taking on the new nature we have in Christ. Israel got out of Egypt the day they partook of the Passover, but it still took years to get Egypt out of them. They were saved from their slavery to Egypt in a day, but it took much longer to save them from the slave nature. We too are free from the authority of this present evil age the moment we believe in the cross of Jesus for our atonement, but it still takes a while longer to get free of the old nature.

Getting free is a process that begins with our new birth. At birth, we begin the process of maturity and becoming what we are to be. The same is true when we are born again. Then we must embrace the transformation addressed in Romans 12:1-2, which is compared to the changes a caterpillar undergoes when it becomes a butterfly. The greatest struggle for the creature is breaking out of the cocoon, but it is that struggle by which it builds the strength to flap those large wings. This too is the purpose for the struggle we go through in throwing off our old nature and taking on the new—it strengthens us to be able to handle the authority we are given in our new nature.

Fellow Workers

2:19-30: True New Testament ministry is team ministry. Paul was always mindful of the team of workers he was joined to. He did not just mention their contribution to the work, but shared how deeply they were bonded together in Christ and were essential for the work of the Lord.

NOTES

Paul's Letter to the
PHILIPPIANS
Philippians 3

Our Credentials

1 Finally, my brethren, rejoice in the Lord. To write the same things to you is not bothersome to me, but is for your safety.

2 Beware of the dogs, beware of the evil workers, beware of the circumcision.

3 We are the true circumcision, who worship by the Spirit of God, and glory in Christ Jesus, and put no confidence in the flesh,

4 though I myself might have confidence even in the flesh. In fact, if any man thinks he can have confidence in the flesh, I could even more.

5 I was circumcised on the eighth day. I am an Israelite by birth, of the tribe of Benjamin, and a Hebrew of Hebrews. As to the law, I was a Pharisee.

6 As for zeal, I persecuted the church, and according to the righteousness that is in the law, found blameless.

7 Even so what things were gain to me, these have I counted loss for Christ.

8 Yes truly, I count all things to be loss for the excellency of the knowledge of Christ Jesus my Lord. Indeed, I suffered the loss of all things, and do count them but rubbish so that I may gain Christ,

9 and be found in Him, not having a righteousness of my own, even that which is of the law, but that which is through faith in Christ, the righteousness that is from God by faith,

10 that I may know Him, and the power of His resurrection, and the fellowship of His sufferings, becoming conformed to His death,

11 so that I may attain to the resurrection from the dead.

The High Calling

12 Not that I have already obtained, or have already been made perfect, but I press on in order to lay hold on that for which I was laid hold of by Christ Jesus.

13 Brethren, I do not consider that I have yet attained, but this one thing I do, forgetting the things that are behind, I look forward to the things that are ahead.

14 I press on toward the goal of the prize of the high calling of God in Christ Jesus.

True and False Workers

15 Let us therefore, as many as are mature be thus minded. If in anything you have a different perspective God will also reveal this to you.

16 Only, let us walk by the same standard to which we have obtained.

17 Brethren, together be imitators of me, and mark those who walk as the example that you have in us.

18 For many walk, of whom I told you often, and now tell you even weeping, that they are enemies of the cross of Christ.

19 Their end is perdition whose god is their appetite, whose glory is in their shame, and whose minds are on earthly things.

20 For our citizenship is in heaven, from which we also wait for our Savior, the Lord Jesus Christ,

21 who will change and renew the body of our humiliation, that it may be conformed to the body of His glory, according to the authority He has to put all things in subjection to Himself.

Our Credentials

Philippians 3:1-11: When we grasp our identity in Christ, no other human basis of identity, race, culture, profession, or any earthly accomplishments can possibly compare. Paul could have boasted in his Jewish roots as much as anyone, but compared to being in Christ, they were like rubbish to him, something to be cast off. This is offensive to those who have not yet grasped who they are called to be in Christ, but rather seek identity through lesser things. There is a place for respecting our culture and heritage, but once we perceive our calling in Christ, any other identity is so overshadowed that being overly focused on them only reveals how low and natural our vision is.

After making the basis of our identity in Christ clear, Paul begins a remarkable discourse about our high calling in Christ and what he is doing to attain it. When Paul writes that he is seeking to be conformed to the image of the Lord's death so that he might attain to the resurrection from the dead, this could have been translated the "better resurrection," which is also spoken of in Hebrews.

Paul had eternal life and was guaranteed resurrection the moment he believed in Christ for the atonement of his sin. This "better resurrection" is the high calling in Christ that has been the pursuit of the greatest souls to ever walk the earth. It is the calling to be sons and daughters of God and joint heirs with Christ. This high calling is not gained just by believing in the Lord for our atonement. It is a race to be won, a pursuit so great that, as this great apostle declared, any other identity or attainment is but rubbish in comparison.

The High Calling

3:12-14: As Paul elaborates on this high calling, he says that he does not yet consider that he has attained to it. Paul was one of the greatest apostles of all time, yet he saw something so high that after one of the most important and fruitful ministries of all time, he was still pressing on to the goal of this high calling. If this was the case with Paul, how could anyone claim to have attained it in this life? Those who consider that they have already attained have succumbed to the pride that will cause all on this path to stumble. Stay humble.

It is likely that we cannot know in this life if we have attained to the high calling. However, we can know with certainty that we have attained eternal life in Christ, and even the lowest person in the kingdom will be in awe at the glory and wonders of the life to come. Even so, this discourse makes it clear that there is a high calling, and that it is the greatest pursuit there could ever be in this life.

True and False Workers

3:15-21: The true Christian life is not about what we attain to. It is, like Christ's own life, a life of daily sacrifice. Discipleship is a life of the cross, not seeking our own, but the laying down of our lives to save the lost. The call is to seek the glory of Christ in all things, not our own recognition or glory. Those who pursue ministry as a means of self-promotion, for attaining their own goals, are false workers. There is a difference between pursuing ministry as a profession and pursuing it as a calling. We must distinguish between these by recognizing the self-promoting ones who are not living the life of the cross and reject them as ministers, while honoring and supporting those who are true servants of the King.

NOTES

Paul's Letter to the
PHILIPPIANS
Philippians 4

Standing Fast, Walking True

1. Therefore my brethren, beloved and longed for, my joy and crown, stand fast in the Lord my beloved.

2. I exhort Euodia, and I exhort Syntyche, to be of the same mind in the Lord.

3. Yes, I beseech you as true yoke fellows, help these women, for they labored with me in the gospel, with Clement also, and the rest of my fellow workers, whose names are in the book of life.

4. Rejoice in the Lord always, and again I will say, "Rejoice!"

5. Let your patience be made known to all men. The Lord is at hand.

6. Be anxious for nothing, but in everything by prayer and supplication, with thanksgiving, let your requests be made known to God,

7. and the peace of God that surpasses all understanding will guard your hearts and your minds in Christ Jesus.

8. Finally, brethren, whatever things are true, whatever things are honorable, whatever things are just, whatever things are pure, whatever things are lovely, whatever things are good, if there is any virtue, and if there is any praise, think on these things.

9. The things that you both learned and received, and heard and saw in me, these things do: and the God of peace will be with you.

10. I rejoice in the Lord greatly, that now at length you have revived your care for me. Of course, you always did think of me, but you lacked the opportunity to do something for me.

The Patient Heart

11 Not that I speak of this because of my needs because I have learned to be content in whatever state I am in.

12 I know how to be abased, and I also know how to abound. In everything, and in all things, I have learned the secret both of going hungry, or being filled, to abound or to be in need.

13 I can do all things through Christ who strengthens me.

14 Even so, you did well to share in the fellowship of my affliction.

15 As you Philippians know, that in the beginning of my service to the gospel, when I departed from Macedonia, no church had fellowship with me in the matter of giving and receiving except you.

16 In Thessalonica you sent more than once to my take care of my needs.

Our Account in Heaven

17 Not that I seek for the gift, but I seek for the fruit that increases to your account.

18 I have all things, and I abound. I am filled, having received from Epaphroditus the things that came from you, and aroma of a sweet smell, an acceptable sacrifice, well pleasing to God.

19 My God will supply all of your needs according to His riches in glory in Christ Jesus.

20 Now to our God and Father be the glory for ever and ever. Amen.

21 Salute every saint in Christ Jesus. The brethren that are with me salute you.

22 All the saints salute you, especially those who are of Caesar's household.

23 The grace of the Lord Jesus Christ be with your spirit.

Standing Fast, Walking True

Philippians 4:1-10: Paul begins to close this letter by acknowledging and honoring his fellow workers in the gospel, which he is always considerate to do. Then he lays out a simple formula for how to walk daily in Christ Jesus. This begins with rejoicing. As we are told in Psalm 100, we enter the Lord's gates

with thanksgiving. Being a thankful person is the primary way we enter and abide in His presence.

Then Paul warns about anxiety—the primary way that we depart from faith and the presence of the Lord. Anxiety is the fear that we have a situation that is too big for the Lord and is a basic departure from faith. In contrast to this, if we turn to the Lord in faith with prayer, then His peace will guard our hearts and minds in Him. Peace is the first sign that one is abiding in Christ.

After this, the great apostle exhorts believers to keep their minds on things that are good and true. "In the world you have tribulation," but the world is not where our hearts and minds are to be fixed. We are commanded to keep seeking the things that are above. This does not mean that we are not to keep in touch with issues of this world or the enemy's schemes. We are told not to be ignorant of these. However, when our hope, faith, and attention are on the kingdom, then even the worst crises in this world will not cause anxiety because we are abiding in a kingdom that cannot be shaken.

Then Paul commends the Philippians for being considerate of his needs and sending provisions for him. Of course, Paul was thankful that they would care that much for him, but this also is a sign of their maturity in Christ. To see growing maturity in those they are ministering to is most encouraging for any laborer in the gospel.

The Patient Heart

4:11-16: Paul learned that when he was being abased, it was an opportunity to grow in Christ, and when he was abounding, it was an opportunity to grow in Christ. Whatever state he was in was a good one. So is it with us.

The apostle concludes with the reminder that he can "do all things through Christ." So can we. There is nothing that He has allowed in our lives that will tempt us beyond what we can bear. There is nothing that He does not intend to lead us to victory in. Whatever He has allowed into our lives, we know there will be triumph and that it will work for our good. We should also note that Paul states this in relation to enduring times of being abased or in need. These trials are for our maturity and strengthening. We must learn to embrace and use them as Paul did.

Our Account in Heaven

4:17-23: After commending the Philippians for sending provision for his needs, Paul affirms that this has increased their account in heaven. We do have accounts in heaven that we make deposits into and withdrawals from. There is no greater investment we could ever make, or a safer one, than what we invest in the kingdom.

NOTES

Paul's Letter to The Philippians Proper Names and Definitions

Benjamin: son of the right hand
Christ: anointed
Clement: mild; good; merciful
Epaphroditus: agreeable; handsome
Euodias: sweet scent
Hebrews: descendants of Heber
Israel: who prevails with God
Jesus: Savior; Deliverer
Macedonia: burning; adoration
Paul: small; little
Pharisees: set apart
Philippi: warlike; a lover of horses
Syntyche: that speaks or discourses
Thessalonica: victory against the Thessalonians
Timothy: honor of God; valued by God

INTRODUCTION
Paul's Letter to the Colossians

This Epistle was written by Paul while he was in Rome during his first imprisonment. This is recorded in Acts 28 and is estimated to have been between A.D. 57 and 62.

Like some of Paul's other letters, this Epistle was written in response to information he received about the church in Colossae. Paul's main purpose was to encourage this church about their spiritual maturity and to encourage them to continue to adhere to the preeminence and centrality of Christ. The apostle commended them for the good reputation they had attained. He then refuted some false doctrines and legalism being promoted there. As was also Paul's custom, after addressing the doctrinal issues, he leaves them with good practical wisdom.

For eloquence, as well as concise and profound teaching, especially in the description of the stature of Christ in creation, this is one of Paul's preeminent Epistles. It also reveals that most, if not all, of the churches of that time, as well as today, go through the same pattern of attacks on their faith and on the sound doctrine they were established on.

This is one reason why churches that are part of networks or that are under the oversight of apostolic ministries or teams seem to do so much better in combating these false teachings. This is because they have access to counsel and help that independent works may not have. Even so, the main defense against any attack, opposition, or trial is to be joined to the Head, Jesus Christ, and remain obedient to Him in all things.

Paul's Letter to the
COLOSSIANS
Colossians 1

Salutation and Commendation

1 Paul, an apostle of Christ Jesus by the will of God, and Timothy our brother,

2 to the saints and faithful brethren in Christ who are at Colossae: Grace to you, and peace from God our Father.

3 We give thanks to God the Father of our Lord Jesus Christ, praying always for you,

4 having heard of your faith in Christ Jesus, and your love toward all the saints.

5 We know this is because of the hope that is laid up for you in the heavens, which you heard before in the word of the truth that is the gospel.

6 This has come to you, even as it is also throughout the world, bearing fruit and increasing, as it does in you also since the day you heard and knew the grace of God in truth.

7 You also learned about Epaphras, our beloved fellow servant, who is a faithful minister of Christ on our behalf,

8 and who also declared to us your love in the Spirit.

The Glorious Life

9 For this cause we also, since the day we heard it, do not cease to pray and make a request for you, that you may be filled with the knowledge of His will in all spiritual wisdom and understanding,

10 and that you may walk in a manner worthy of the Lord, pleasing Him in all things, bearing fruit in every good work, and increasing in the knowledge of God,

11 strengthened with all power, according to the power of His glory, in all patience and endurance with joy.

12 We give thanks to the Father, who made us able to be partakers of the inheritance of the saints in light, and

13 who delivered us out of the power of darkness, and translated us into the kingdom of the Son in which we know His love.

The Glorious Son

14 It is in Him that we have our redemption, and the forgiveness of our sins.

15 He is the image of the invisible God, the firstborn of all creation.

16 For in Him were all things created, in the heavens and upon the earth, things visible and invisible, whether thrones or dominions, or principalities, or powers, all things have been created through Him, and for Him.

17 He is before all things, and in Him all things hold together.

18 He is the Head of the body, the church, who is the beginning, the firstborn from the dead, that in all things He might have the preeminence.

19 For it was the Father's good pleasure that in Him should all the fullness dwell,

20 and through Him to reconcile all things to Himself, having made peace through the blood of His cross, through Him, whether things upon the earth, or things in the heavens.

The Glorious Gospel

21 So you, being in time past alienated, and enemies in your mind and in your evil works,

22 yet now has He reconciled in the body of His flesh through death, to present you holy and without blemish, and without reproach before Him,

23 if you continue in the faith, grounded and steadfast, and not moved away from the hope of the gospel which you heard, that was preached in all creation under heaven, and for which I, Paul, was made a minister.

24 Now I rejoice in my sufferings for your sake, and complete my part of that which was left behind of the afflictions of Christ. I do this in my flesh for His body's sake, which is the church.

25 For this reason I was made a minister, according to the dispensation of God that was given to me for you to fulfill the word of God.

26 This mystery has been hidden for ages, from other generations, but now has been made known to His saints,

27 to whom God was pleased to make known what are the riches of the glory of this mystery among the Gentiles, that is Christ in you, the hope of glory.

28 It is Him that we proclaim, admonishing every man and teaching every man in all wisdom so that we may present every man complete in Christ.

29 Therefore I labor, striving according to His power that works mightily through me.

Salutation and Commendation

Colossians 1:1-8: As is common in Paul's letters, his salutation is full of encouragement and praise for the church he is writing to. In this case, it is to a church that Paul never visited. He knew this church by the reputation of their faith in Christ Jesus and the love they had for the saints (v.4).

The Glorious Life

1:9-13: This is one of the greatest summaries found in The Bible of what should be the basic devotion of every believer—knowing Christ Jesus and living for Him. There is no greater

adventure, no greater cause, than to follow the King and do His will.

The Glorious Son

1:14-20: This is one of the most clear and basic statements of Christology found in The Bible. He is the Creator and the Purpose for the Creation. All things will be summed up in Him, and that is the ultimate purpose of our lives—to be found in Him, grow up into Him, and glorify His name on the earth.

The Glorious Gospel

1:21-29: This extraordinary chapter continues with a beautiful description of the majesty of the gospel and Paul's apostolic mandate to preach it among the Gentiles.

Then Paul states what may be the concise purpose of the apostolic ministry and indeed all ministry—to present every man complete in Christ. It seems that Paul lived this devotion like few others have. When he met someone, he would first discern their spiritual state, and if they did not know the Lord, he would introduce them. If they were believers, he would seek to give them something that would help them mature in Him, always laboring to bring forth Christ in His people.

NOTES

Paul's Letter to the
COLOSSIANS
Colossians 2

The Centrality of Christ

1 I would have you to know how greatly I strive for you, and for those who are at Laodicea, and for as many as have not seen my face in the flesh,

2 so that their hearts may be comforted, being knit together in love, and with all the riches of the full assurance of understanding, that they may know the mystery of God, even Christ.

3 It is in Him that are hidden all the treasures of wisdom and knowledge.

4 This I say, that no one may delude you with persuasive speech.

5 For though I am absent in the flesh, yet I am with you in the spirit, enjoying and beholding your order, and the steadfastness of your faith in Christ.

6 Therefore, as you received Christ Jesus the Lord, so walk in Him,

7 being rooted and built up in Him, established in your faith, even as you were taught, abounding in thanksgiving.

8 Take heed lest there would be any one that takes you as their spoil through their philosophy and vain deceit, after the tradition of men, after the elementary principles of the world, and not according to Christ.

The Victory of The Cross

9 For in Him dwells all the fullness of the Godhead bodily,

10 and in Him you are made complete, who is the Head over all principalities and powers.

11 It is in Him that you were also circumcised with a circumcision not made with hands, in the putting off of the body of the flesh, which is the circumcision of Christ.

12 We have been buried with Him through baptism, and you were also raised with Him through faith in the work of God, who raised Him from the dead.

13 You, being dead through your trespasses and the un-circumcision of your flesh, did He make alive together with Him, having forgiven us all of our trespasses,

14 having blotted out the bond written in ordinances that was held against us, He has removed it by nailing it to the cross.

15 On the cross He spoiled the principalities and the powers, He made an open show of them, triumphing over them.

The Deception of Legalism

16 Let no man therefore judge you in what you eat or drink, or in regard to a feast day, or a new moon, or a Sabbath day,

17 which are all shadows of the things to come, but the body is Christ's.

18 Let no man rob you of your prize by a devotion to self-abasement, or the worshiping of the angels, or becoming prideful because of visions they have seen, being puffed up by their fleshly mind,

19 and not holding fast to the Head, from whom the whole body, being supplied and knit together through the joints and ligaments, increases with the increase of God.

20 If you died with Christ to the elementary principles of the world, why, as though still living in the world, do you subject yourselves to ordinances like,

21 do not handle, do not taste, and do not touch?

22 All of these are things destined to perish with the using, after the precepts and doctrines of men.

23 These teachings do have an appearance of wisdom in worshiping our own will, self-abasement, and the severe treatment of the body, but they are of no value against the indulgence of the flesh.

The Centrality of Christ

Colossians 2:1-8: In this chapter, the apostle begins to make a transition from describing the glory of Christ and the calling of believers to refuting the false teachings and legalism assaulting this church. However, he always keeps Christ Himself as our focus and devotion.

The Victory of The Cross

2:9-15: Paul reaffirms the ultimate foundation of all spiritual truth—the victory of the cross and what it accomplished for us, and for all of creation, triumphing over every spiritual enemy.

The Deception of Legalism

2:16-23: This important exhortation warns against esteeming spiritual experiences over basic devotion to Christ and sound doctrine. Only when we are rooted and grounded in Christ will we be able to interpret and apply such experiences properly. When we base our relationship to God on our devotion and works rather than on the cross of Jesus, it is an affront to the cross and leads to other basic and destructive deceptions.

NOTES

Paul's Letter to the Colossians

Colossians 3

Live in The Spirit

1 If then, you were raised together with Christ, seek the things above, where Christ is seated on the right hand of God.

2 Set your mind on the things above, not on the things that are upon the earth.

3 For you died, and your life is hidden with Christ in God.

4 When Christ, who is our life, will be manifested, then you will also be manifested in glory with Him.

Die to The Flesh

5 Therefore put to death that which is earthly, such as fornication, uncleanness, passion, evil desire, and covetousness, that is idolatry.

6 It is because of these things that the wrath of God will come upon the sons of disobedience.

7 In these things you also once walked, when you lived this way,

8 but now you put them all away, including anger, wrath, malice, railing, and shameful speaking.

9 Do not lie to one another, seeing that you have put off the old man with his evil doings,

10 and have put on the new man that is being renewed by knowledge of the One that created him.

Our Unity Through Christ

11 In Him there cannot be a distinction between Greek and Jew, circumcision and un-circumcision, barbarian, Scythian, bondman, freeman, but Christ is all, and in all.

12 Therefore, as God's elect, holy and beloved, put on a heart of compassion, kindness, lowliness, meekness, longsuffering,

13 always being patient with one another, forgiving each other, if any man has a complaint against anyone. Just as the Lord forgave you, so must you forgive others.

14 Above all things put on love, which is the perfect bond of unity.

15 Let the peace of Christ rule in your hearts, to which also you were called as one body. Always be thankful.

16 Let the word of Christ dwell in you richly, in all wisdom, teaching and admonishing one another with psalms and hymns and spiritual songs, singing to God with grace in your hearts.

17 Whatever you do, in word or in deed, do all in the name of the Lord Jesus, giving thanks to God the Father through Him.

Instructions for The Family

18 Wives, be subject to your husbands, as is fitting in the Lord.

19 Husbands, love your wives, and do not be embittered towards them.

20 Children, obey your parents in all things, for this is very pleasing to the Lord.

21 Fathers, do not provoke your children, so that they will not be discouraged.

Instructions for Workers and Masters

22 Servants, obey those who are your masters according to the flesh, in all things, not just to be seen as men-pleasers, but with a single-minded devotion from your heart as unto the Lord.

23 Whatever you do, do your work with all of your heart as unto the Lord, not men.

24 Know that it is from the Lord that you will receive your wages, and an inheritance, because you serve the Lord Christ.

25 For he that does wrong will receive the wages of that wrong that he has done, for there is no respect of persons in this.

26 Masters, render to your servants that which is just and equal, knowing that you also have a Master in heaven.

Live in The Spirit

Colossians 3:1-4: It was the apostolic resolve to counter the false with the true. Paul's remedy for false mysticism that was creeping into this church was to exhort them to adhere to the true mysticism of Christ, abiding with the Lord in the spiritual realm. He then makes the distinction between true and false mysticism: false mysticism is self-centered, building on pride and focused on what we can attain, while true mysticism is Christ-centered, seeking to abide and grow in Him, seeking His glory, not our own.

Die to The Flesh

3:5-10: Countering the false religious spirit of legalism that was also creeping into this church, Paul exhorts them to the true and simple obligation of dying to the old nature in order to live in the new creation. Legalism seeks to have us base our relationship to God on what we do. However, new creation people are members of God's family—sons and daughters—who do good works from a position of having God's approval, not in order to seek it. Legalism is self-centered and builds on the pride of what we do, but life in the Spirit is Christ-centered and based on what He did for us.

Our Unity Through Christ

3:11-17: Paul brilliantly and simply confronts the evil of racism. He follows that with a powerful exhortation to live by the higher ways of the Spirit, summed up by the perfect unity we have when we walk in love.

Instructions for The Family

3:18-21: These four verses contain more wisdom for a strong family life than many books that have been written.

Instructions for Workers and Masters

3:22-26: These five verses contain some of the greatest council for labor relations ever written. In modern terms, the "master" would be our supervisor or boss.

NOTES

Paul's Letter to the
COLOSSIANS
Colossians 4

Request for Prayer, Grace and Wisdom

1 Continue steadfastly in prayer, being a watchman, always giving thanks.

2 Pray for us also, that God may open to us a door for the word, to speak the mystery of Christ, for which I am also in bonds.

3 Pray that I may be clear when I speak.

4 Walk in wisdom toward those who are outside of the faith, redeeming the time.

5 Let your speech always be with grace, seasoned with salt, that you may know how you should answer each one.

Paul's Co-laborers

6 Tychicus shall make known to you all of my affairs, who is a beloved brother, faithful minister, and fellow-servant in the Lord.

7 I have sent him to you for this very purpose, that you may know our state, and that he may comfort your hearts.

8 He is together with Onesimus, the faithful and beloved brother, who is one of your own. They will make known to you all things that are done here.

9 Aristarchus, my fellow-prisoner, salutes you, as well as Mark, the cousin of Barnabas, about whom you received instructions that if he comes to you, receive him,

10 along with Jesus that is called Justus, who is also of the circumcision. These are my fellow-workers in the kingdom of God, men that have been a comfort to me.

11 Epaphras, who is one of you, a servant of Christ Jesus, salutes you, always striving for you in his prayers, that you may stand perfect and fully assured in all the will of God.

12 For I bear him witness, that he has much labor for you, and for those in Laodicea, and for those in Hierapolis.

13 Luke, the beloved physician, and Demas salute you.

14 Salute the brethren that are in Laodicea, and Nymphas, and the church that is in their house.

15 When this epistle has been read among you, have it read also in the church of the Laodiceans, and you also read the epistle from Laodicea.

16 Say to Archippus, "Take heed to the ministry that you have received in the Lord, and fulfill it."

17 This salutation is by me, Paul, written with my own hand. Remember my bonds. Grace be with you.

Request for Prayer, Grace and Wisdom

Colossians 4:1-5: In his conclusion, Paul exhorts the saints to pray as watchmen. In the Old Testament, this was one of the terms given to prophets who were posted on the spiritual ramparts of Israel to watch over the soul of the nation. This is one of the crucial ministries of the church, yet on the local level it is rarely recognized and implemented. Many of our troubles could be avoided if those who are given to the body for this purpose were recognized and placed as they should be in every congregation.

Paul's Co-laborers

4:6-17: Paul's emphasis on his co-workers reveals how deeply he was committed to their ministry together as a team. Basic New Testament ministry is a team ministry. Those who do not operate in the team of equipping ministries named in Ephesians 4 will be limited at best.

Paul's Letter to The Colossians Proper Names and Definitions

Archippus: a master of horses
Aristarchus: the best prince
Barnabas: son of the prophet, or of consolation
Christ: anointed
Demas: popular
Epaphras: covered with foam
Gentiles: the nations or pagan
Hierapolis: holy city
Jesus: Savior, Deliverer, Yahweh is salvation
Jew: the praise of the Lord, confession
Justus: just or upright
Laodicea: just people
Luke: luminous, white
Mark: polite, shining
Nymphas: spouse, bridegroom
Onesimus: profitable, useful
Paul: small, little
Psalms: songs of praise
Tychicus: casual, by chance

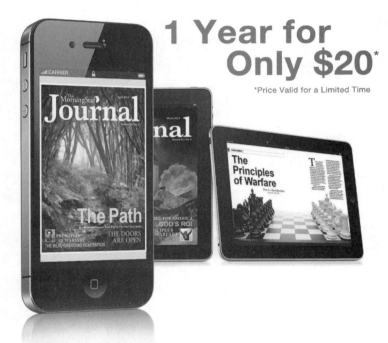

NOW FEATURING WORK EDUCATIONAL PROGRAM

MorningStar University

SCHOOL OF THEOLOGY AND DOCTRINE   SCHOOL OF THE HOLY SPIRIT   SCHOOL OF MISSIONS

RELEASING A SUPERNATURAL ARMY TO TRANSFORM THE WORLD

BUILD STRONG BIBLICAL FOUNDATIONS AND A CHRISTIAN WORLDVIEW

GAIN PRACTICAL AND SUPERNATURAL TOOLS FOR SUCCESS

ENGAGE IN "SPECIAL FORCES" MISSION OPPORTUNITIES

INTERN WITH INTERNATIONAL MINISTRY, EDUCATION, AND BUSINESS LEADERS

1, 2, AND 3 YEAR PROGRAMS AVAILABLE
* ASSOCIATE DEGREES AVAILABLE

NOW ACCEPTING APPLICATIONS

KNOW THE LORD   IMPACT HISTORY   CHANGE THE WORLD

FOR MORE INFORMATION

CALL: 803-802-5544, EXTENSION 238
VISIT: WWW.MORNINGSTARUNIVERSITY.COM
EMAIL: MSUOFFICE@MORNINGSTARMINISTRIES.ORG